# PAUL

## HIS LIFE AND WORK

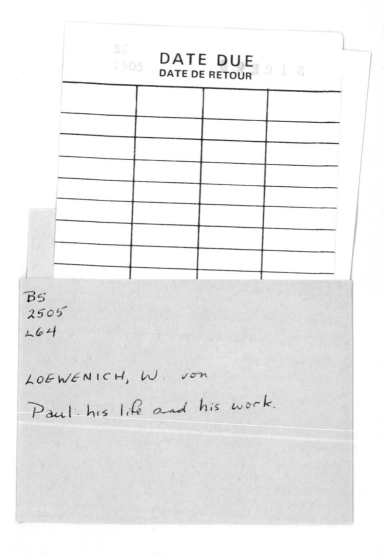

# WALTHER von LOEWENICH

# PAUL

## HIS LIFE AND WORK

Translated by
GORDON E. HARRIS

OLIVER AND BOYD
EDINBURGH AND LONDON
1960

OLIVER AND BOYD LTD

Tweeddale Court
Edinburgh I

39A Welbeck Street
London W.1.

This book is a translation of the second German edition of
*Paulus: Sein Leben und Werk*, by Walther von Loewenich,
first published by Luther Verlag, Ruhr 1949.

Except where otherwise stated, all Scripture quotations
in this book are from the Revised Standard Version of
the Bible, copyright 1946 and 1952 by the Division of
Christian Education, National Council of the Churches
of Christ in the U.S.A., and used by permission.

ENGLISH EDITION
First published 1960

PRINTED IN GREAT BRITAIN FOR OLIVER AND BOYD LTD
BY ROBERT CUNNINGHAM AND SONS LTD, LONGBANK WORKS, ALVA

OSKAR GRETHER
✝ 3rd August 1949

*in memoriam*

# PREFACE TO THE FIRST EDITION

THE chief need in our churches today is for a deepened knowledge of the Bible. But even the best intentions often founder on the difficulties which the Bible presents to the modern reader's understanding. This applies not least to the world of Paul's ideas. Evangelical Christianity is indissolubly bound up with it; but where, apart from scholarly circles, is it really known and understood? Our book is intended to render a service in this respect. Accordingly, it does not content itself with describing the truly heroic life of the Apostle; it also attempts, by means of an introduction to his letters, to awaken an understanding of Pauline ideas. This assumes, of course, that the reader will refer to the New Testament for himself; and if this book enables him to do so profitably, then it will have fulfilled its object. Today, Paul is being attacked from all sides; once a man has encountered him, however, he finds it impossible ever to break away.

*Erlangen*                                                    WALTHER VON LOEWENICH

## PREFACE TO THE SECOND EDITION

In response to many requests, it has been decided that there should be a new edition of my book on Paul, which has been out of print for a long time. Apart from a number of factual corrections, this edition is substantially the same as the earlier one. The ideological front surveyed in the first edition has collapsed. But our churches today are no less in need of a true understanding of what the work of the apostle Paul means for the Church of Jesus Christ.

*Erlangen*                                                    WALTHER VON LOEWENICH

# CONTENTS

# PAUL: FOR AND AGAINST

FEW figures in history have known so much love and veneration with, at the same time, so much hatred and misunderstanding as the apostle Paul. It was already so during his lifetime; and this fate, which has pursued him through the centuries, has become apparent again today. Paul was regarded by the Jews of his time as the great apostate; he, upon whom they had placed so many hopes, had gone over to the other camp, and for this he was rewarded with fanatical hatred. The newly converted Paul encountered mistrust and misunderstanding even in his own ranks. His zeal appeared too daring, his genius too precipitate, to be grasped by the simpler and slower Christians. The New Testament gives us evidence of this state of affairs. "False apostles" (II Cor. XI.13) travel behind the great Apostle of the Gentiles, and sow overnight the weeds of doubt and envy in the young churches. The writer of the Epistle of James deems it necessary to warn against the Pauline doctrine of Justification by faith alone (II.14ff.), and even the Second Epistle of Peter (III.15f.) speaks benevolently but apprehensively of the intellectual difficulty of Paul's letters, and of the misuse to which they are put.

By contrast, however, we have from about the same period evidences of the most eager respect. Already in the Acts of the Apostles Paul is the great apostle of the nations who is seen as a parallel to Peter, the prince of the apostles. About the turn of the century the letter of the Roman presbyter Clement honours the "good apostles," Peter and Paul. Of the latter he writes: "Seven times he was in bonds, he was exiled, he was stoned, he was a herald both in the East and in the West, he gained the noble fame of his faith, he taught righteousness to all the world, and when he had reached the limits of the West he gave his testimony before the rulers, and thus passed from the world and was taken into the Holy Place,—the greatest example of endurance."[1]

---

[1] I Clem. (*i.e.* Clement's first Epistle to the Corinthians), v; tr. Kirsopp Lake in *The Apostolic Fathers*, Loeb classical Library, 2 vols., London 1912 (repr. 1945), VOL. I, p. 17.

I

The Christians in Ephesus can regard it as the very highest compliment when the martyr-bishop Ignatius designates them in his letter to the Ephesians as "fellow-initiates with Paul, who was sanctified, who gained a good report, who was right blessed, in whose footsteps may I be found when I shall attain to God, who in every epistle makes mention of you in Christ Jesus."[2]

The authority of the Apostle certainly stands firm in the churches a generation after his death; but at the same time the anxious statement in II Peter turned out to be true. Misconceptions regarding Paul increased at the same rate as his standing. That applies even to the Epistle of Clement, which has already been mentioned. When Luther said that the deviation from the Pauline message first took place in the medieval Church, he was cherishing a happy illusion: it can be established even in the generation after Paul. Certainly Paul was becoming increasingly honoured, but also less understood. The story of Pauline interpretation in the early Church is, in fact, a story of misrepresentation all along the line. Though the arch-heretic Marcion, the only "Paulinist" of the second century, completely misunderstood his master, Paul did at least stimulate him to activity. In no other instance, however, did such misunderstanding even produce activity. The Pauline teaching had lost its power as leaven: in being canonised Paul was also catholicised.

Yet the embers of Pauline Christianity were still glowing under the ashes, waiting for the wind of the Spirit to fan the spark into a flame. It was the autumn of the year 386. In a garden in Milan a man whose soul had rubbed against the deepest spiritual problems was struggling with the most difficult decision of his life. A child's voice rang out in the midst like a call from heaven: "Take and read." The eye of the seeker fell upon Rom. XIII.13-14. The decision was made. Augustine became a Christian. Is it chance that a word of Paul provided the final impetus? At the hour of his conversion Augustine had not yet perceived the true content of the Pauline message. But it disclosed itself more and more to him in the course of his life as a Christian. To him, the message of

---

[2] Ignatius, Epistle to the Ephesians, ch. xii; tr. Kirsopp Lake in *The Apostolic Fathers*, VOL. I, p. 187.

"grace alone" was no dead doctrine, but became the very key to his existence. Augustine thus became Paul's first great pupil, and his theology the first impressive formulation that the preaching of the Apostle to the Gentiles found in Church doctrine.

Truly, the disciple is not above his master. The fate of Paulinism attached also to Augustinism. Although Augustine was honoured, his sublime figure was forced into the framework of conventional ecclesiastical thought. All the sharp edges and corners were smoothed away; and it was precisely the Pauline element in Augustine's teaching which was thereby affected. In the Middle Ages both of them, Paul and his pupil Augustine, rose to the very highest saintly honours. From the pillars of mighty cathedrals they looked down in greeting; but they did not descend into the teeming life of men. The uncanny explosive power of their ideas was cautiously built into carefully-prepared systems, while simpler recipes were prepared for practical piety. The fate that Paulinism experienced in the early Church before Augustine recurred to an even higher degree in the medieval Church.

All the greater therefore was the resurrection that it was to experience at the beginning of the modern era. If Paulinism was for Augustine only one, even though the most remarkable, of the forces which affected his spiritual existence, for Luther it was the point of departure and it was always to remain the centre of his theology and piety. Here again it was shaped by the most private personal experience, but quite differently from Augustine. In the case of Augustine's conversion any other text could, humanly speaking, equally well have brought about his decision. Luther, on the other hand, brooded day and night, as he himself says, over the interpretation of a passage from Paul, that is, over the meaning of Rom. 1.16-17. This passage was not just picked out at random, for it contains and sums up the central theme of the Pauline message. Luther came to Paul with the great question of his life; once Paul had given him his answer he remained his lifelong disciple. Yet there is still more to be said. Luther was stirred by fundamentally the same question as that with which Paul had struggled: How do I become righteous in the sight of God? The fact that they had this question in common led at this juncture to a fertilisation of theological thinking and practical piety by Paulinism, as is nowhere else to be demonstrated in the history of the Church. Reformed Christianity is Paulinism resurrected to an unparalleled extent. The starting-point in experience of this highly remarkable occurrence in the history of religion has proved to be so powerful that not even its formulation into propositions has led to any theological rigidity or real atrophy. The Pauline leaven has so permeated the doctrine of the Evangelical Church that it has never been possible since to remove it completely. The fate of Augustine's teaching has never been repeated in Lutheranism. Naturally deviations have not failed to occur from time to time, but the power of recalling origins was always great enough to prevent any complete and lasting departure. Paul remained the apostle of Protestantism, just as Luther remains the greatest disciple of Paul. His mighty figure, conceived in such impressive proportions by Albrecht Dürer as a symbolic expression of the new righteousness, towers over the centuries to come as a living admonisher. It has been impossible to avoid him ever since; the only two alternatives that remain are grateful love and burning hatred.

Not only in the recent past but even at present, the Apostle has had his share of both. Even historical learning, which has busied itself fully with Paul, could not avoid making a verdict for or against him. One can no more be neutral about the Pauline message than one can about a fire that is spreading in all directions. If that applies to the representatives of scholarship, it applies even more to men who wished to help in moulding the spiritual future of the German people. Let us quote the testimony of just two of these men.

Paul de Lagarde[3] describes Paul as "completely without vocation." According to him, "Paul, a true descendant of Abraham and, even after his conversion, a Pharisee of Pharisees, possesses no reliable knowledge of Jesus and His Gospel at all. It is therefore "unheard-of that historically-educated men should attach any importance to this man Paul." Even today the Church is suffering mortally from its Pauline heritage. "Paul brought the Old Testament into the Church; and its influence has, so far as is possible, destroyed the Gospel. It was

[3] Paul de Lagarde, *Deutsche Schriften*, Göttingen 1920.

Paul who blessed us with the Pharisaic exposition of Scripture which can prove everything by anything, which comes with the meaning to be found in the text already in its pocket, and then boasts of keeping strictly to the letter. It was Paul who imported the Jewish sacrificial theory, with all its trappings. The whole Jewish view of history . . . was imposed upon us by him. All this he did amidst the lively opposition of the early Church, which, however Jewish it was, thought in less Jewish terms than Paul and at least did not regard a refined 'Israelitism' as a divinely-sent Gospel. Paul's eventual armour against all objections was the theory of 'hardening' derived from Exodus. This theory renders arguing just an easy matter of dismissing a man who brings forward arguments and desires to hear counter-arguments, by means of declaring him to be 'hardened.' " Most of Paul's present-day opponents proceed along the same lines as Lagarde. Even today people are quick to stress the contrast between Jesus and Paul. Paul adulterated the Gospel of Jesus, and this adulteration is seen, just as it was by Lagarde, to take a Judaising form. Here the racial aspects assume, understandably, greater prominence than in Lagarde's case. We have already heard from the latter of the "true descendant of Abraham," and of Paul's "refined Israelitism." It is now alleged that Paul planned nothing less than a Jewish world-revolution, and that, in order to bring it about, he was considering making racial-interbreeding still more prevalent than it already was in the Roman Empire. This man is held responsible for the complete distortion of the pure, genuine teaching of Jesus that is to be found in the so-called Christian Churches, so that, in reality, he is the founder of the Christian Church. To these anti-Pauline thinkers, the "racial decadence" of dying antiquity with all its accompanying evils, together with the "poison of Jewish thought" constitute the unfavourable soil in which the Christian Church has grown; to this day, therefore, she cannot deny her origins. The blame for this development falls first and foremost upon the Jew from Tarsus, whose authority it is important, for that reason, to destroy. Such are the voices which shouted loudest in the ideological propaganda of the "Third Reich."

Let us now hear a witness from the other side: Houston Stewart Chamberlain devotes a whole chapter to Paul in his

book *Mensch und Gott*.[4] Chamberlain, as one of the champions
of a "racial" world-view, also poses, understandably enough,
the question of Paul's Jewish origins. It seems not improbable
to him that Paul may have had a non-Jewish mother; though
here he does admit that it is pure speculation. He finally breaks
off the whole discussion as pointless in order to go on to what
appears to him to be the main issue: "Wherever Paul may have
sprung from, his achievement lies open to our gaze; the primary essence and the primary result of this achievement consists in the fact that he tore Christianity away and separated it
as a new phenomenon from Judaism, thereby becoming the
creator of the Churches, which are in Christ."[5] Chamberlain's
interpretation thus stands in sharpest opposition to that of
Lagarde, with which he was well acquainted. Not the Judaising
of Christianity, but precisely its separation from Judaism: that
is the achievement of Paul, this "fiery spirit from Tarsus."[6]
This break with Judaism had, according to Chamberlain, one
surprising result: the rescue of the primitive Gospel from inevitable destruction.[7] This assertion which is, at first sight,
curious, is substantiated as follows: Jewish Christianity, which
possessed a still-living tradition of Jesus, soon disappeared, as
is well known, from the pages of history. The Gospels would
have been lost with it had they not in the meantime found a
new home among the Gentile Christians won by Paul. Accordingly we owe it to Paul that we still have the Gospel of Jesus.
But is this not vitiated by the fact that Paul, for his part, adulterated the Gospel of Jesus? Chamberlain poses this question
also: "To what extent can we regard Paul as a genuine inter-
preter of the expressed and unexpressed thoughts of Jesus
Christ?"[8] The teaching of Paul certainly contains much that
is alien to the preaching of Jesus. It makes use of images and
conceptions from Jewish apocalyptic and the Hellenistic
mystery-religions, from which one cannot formulate "com-
pulsory dogmas" today. But even for Paul they are only
expedients. "The great, the decisive, the world-shattering
thing about Paul is the manner in which, from various realms

---

[4] Houston Stewart Chamberlain, *Mensch und Gott: Betrachtungen über Religion und Christentum*, 2nd edn., Munich 1923, henceforth cited as *Mensch und Gott*.

[5] *Mensch und Gott*, p. 178.          [6] *Mensch und Gott*, p. 185.

[7] *Mensch und Gott*, p. 184.          [8] *Mensch und Gott*, p. 217.

of the spirit, he collects all that is most likely to impress the
human mind, brings it all into relation with the person of
Jesus Christ, and likewise concentrates all the light in the world
on Him as on a focal point."[9] "Paul perceives the one thing
that is necessary, namely, to lead men to Jesus."[10] In the
Pauline doctrine of Grace, however, a "direct contact"[11] with
Jesus occurs, in addition to which it may also be mentioned
that faith, grace, rebirth and redemption are, in Chamberlain's view, "primitive Aryan concepts."[12]

How is it possible that the testimony of two men who appear
to be so akin in other respects, should sound so different?
Obviously in this matter of the significance to be attached to
Paul we are dealing with a verdict that cannot be reached in
any coldly objective way, but compels one to adopt an individual point of view. That does not mean, however, that the
verdict is a purely arbitrary one. Every man must be able to
produce facts to justify his particular conception of Paul; and
in this case the facts are still, despite numerous difficulties, very
easily ascertained. In many portraits of the Apostle it is not
hard to detect crude distortions attributable not to historical
fact but to the personal revulsion of the author. Hatred can
make a man clear sighted, but more often it blinds him; love,
on the other hand, can make a man blind, but more often it
enables him to see. To love Paul is not for that reason to be
any the less committed to a scrupulous appraisal and representation of historical reality, even where this reality does not seem
to correspond with the ideal. The love which desires the ideal
has still to reach full maturity by Christian standards, for true
love loves not its own image, but the reality, thereby sub-
mitting it to the power of redemption. "Sinners are lovely
because they are loved; they are not loved because they are
lovely" (Luther). The profound saying of the Apostle: "Love
. . . seeketh not its own" (I Cor. XIII.5: R.V.) applies also to
historical investigation.

It is in this sense that we shall sketch a historical picture of
Paul in the following pages. Beforehand, however, it is still
necessary to say a word about the sources from which this
picture may be derived. Here the situation is substantially

---

[9] *Mensch und Gott*, p. 222.    [10] *Mensch und Gott*, p. 223.
[11] *Mensch und Gott*, p. 213.    [12] *Mensch und Gott*, p. 220.

B

more favourable than it is in the search for the historical Jesus. The Lord Jesus Himself left nothing written; the Gospels were not committed to paper until at least a generation after His death. In Paul's case, on the other hand, we possess priceless documents in the form of a whole series of his own letters. Certainly not all those which go under his name are regarded by present-day historical research as genuine letters of Paul. The New Testament preserves for us thirteen of Paul's letters; of these seven are generally acknowledged to be genuine, namely, Romans, I and II Corinthians, Galatians, Philippians, I Thessalonians, and Philemon. The authenticity of II Thessalonians, Ephesians and Colossians, as well as of the so-called Pastoral Epistles (I and II Timothy and Titus) is disputed. In what follows II Thessalonians and Colossians will be accepted as genuine. This does not appear possible where the Pastoral Epistles are concerned, though here opinion is divided. In the previous century men frequently felt obliged to reduce the list of genuine letters even further, but today criticism has become more cautious and conservative. The criteria employed cannot be reviewed in detail here, though something may be said about them at a later stage in our account. One thing only must be emphasised here and now: this criticism did not, nor does it, arise out of malice or unbelief or lack of obedience to the Scriptures, but on the contrary renders possible a more loyal obedience to them and a better historical understanding of the real Paul. As a scientific activity it neither can nor will regard its results as definitive, since, like all scientific judgments, they are subject to vicissitudes. That is no reason, however, for despising such judgments; considering human limitations, remarkable things have been achieved by unwearied industry allied to an undaunted passion for truth and scholarly acumen. In any event, arrogant rejection of this truly great achievement is no sign of Christian humility, nor is fear of unwelcome conclusions consistent with inwardly secure faith.

For the rest, it makes no material difference which particular letters are considered genuine and which not. The outlines of our picture of Paul are determined quite independently. Only the views regarding Paul's end will vary according to one's attitude towards the genuineness or otherwise of the Pastoral Epistles.

In what does the priceless value of Paul's letters consist? Primarily, of course, in the fact that they offer us valuable links with the life of the Apostle. We must take into consideration here the fact that we are dealing with first-hand accounts, and not with a later tradition, although the yield historically and biographically is comparatively slight. It was not Paul's way to talk much about himself and his life. Nevertheless the letters do shed some light upon his destiny. Their chief importance, however, lies in another realm; they are an irreplaceable testimony to Paul's thought and personality.

It would, of course, be quite wrong to look for anything in the nature of a theological system in Paul's letters; all attempts to do so in the past have been somewhat abortive. In a certain sense, naturally, one can call Paul a theologian; but his letters are not so much theological dissertations as writings for particular occasions. They refer mainly to certain specific situations and problems in the churches to which they are addressed, with the result that very different aspects of Paul's thought assume prominence in turn according to the circumstances. One must never forget that the few letters that have been preserved are merely an extract from Paul's life-work. A great deal has certainly been lost, as we happen to know from references to two further letters to the Corinthians. Much that figured prominently in Paul's preaching found no expression in the letters. Above all, however, Paul was no professor who weighed his words carefully before pronouncing, but a smouldering volcano, always liable to erupt. His thinking, for all its typical acuteness, is subject not to the constraint of rules, but to the power of the divine Spirit, which both is and creates life. The thinking of the man who wrote the sentence: "... the letter killeth, but the spirit giveth life" (II Cor. III.6: R.V.), certainly cannot be interpreted "of the letter," but demands to be understood "of the spirit." Consequently, we must not expect his letters to contain a complete system; nevertheless they do contain the volcanic matter of his divinely inspired ideas, and these ideas, wherever they take fire, are still as alive today as ever they were at the beginning.

That is the first thing. At the same time, the letters reflect with the utmost clarity the personality of the Apostle. One expert has asserted that few men of ancient times are so well known to us as Paul, for his letters give us access, as it were, to the depths of his soul, where we can observe its every emotion. These letters are not conscious works of art, they are not "literature" as were, say, the letters of his great contemporary Seneca. Neither were they intended for publication. Probably it never occurred to Paul that they would still be read by anyone after his death. Just as the language of Paul was not the literary Greek of the poets and philosophers but the current vernacular, the so-called *koiné* (*i.e.* common language), so there was nothing at all stilted about his subject-matter. Paul reveals himself in his letters without any restraint. He does not hide himself behind a mask but writes his letters from the heart. And what a man speaks to us here! The tenderest tones are no less typical of him than the most powerful. How this man can blaze with anger, and yet how great is his love! How his spirit can embrace the smallest and the greatest issues with equal devotion! How easy it is to feel behind everything the full weight of his personality! This fact, too, makes these letters, quite apart from their contents, into something sacred which remains significant for all men in all ages.

Thus we have before us in the letters a source of primary importance for an historical understanding of the real Paul. In addition, however, we have a second source: the simple account of the Acts of the Apostles. Without it we should hardly have any clear conception of the actual events of the Apostle's career. It gives us hints as to Paul's origins and his youth; it describes the decisive event of his conversion; above all, it records the separate stages of his activity. Its author, whom we, in accordance with tradition, may well identify as Luke, was for at least part of the time a personal companion of Paul, and possessed, even where he could not give an eyewitness account, some quite reliable source material. One cannot of course regard Acts as historically accurate in all its statements. The speeches which Paul makes in Acts are not verbal transcriptions, but have been shaped by the author after the manner of ancient writers; hence the strong similarity which exists between Paul and Peter in Acts. This is an instance of that temporal detachment from events which makes many things that were originally far more distinct from each other appear in the same dimension. The tensions which stirred the apostolic era inwardly appear more nearly resolved than was the case according to Paul's letters. Thus it is understandable that a certain school of thought should more or less discount Acts as an historical source. Nevertheless, Acts does not merit this summary rejection; in fact, scholarship is now showing signs of movement in the other direction. One cannot accept the data of Acts uncritically; above all, they must be tested as far as possible by reference to Paul's own data. However, one may on the whole make grateful use of them; they can indeed serve to correct certain one-sided impressions arising from the exclusive use of Paul's letters. Next to the letters, then, Acts is as indispensable as ever as a source for the historical understanding of the real Paul.

# TARSUS

"I AM a Jew, from Tarsus in Cilicia, a citizen of no mean city":
thus Paul introduces himself to the Roman tribune on his
imprisonment in Jerusalem (Acts xxi.39; cf. ix.11,
xxii.3). There are no grounds for disputing this statement. It
is worth while, therefore, to look at Paul's home.

The Apostle's judgment of his native city was not exaggerated.
Its natural situation alone made Tarsus a city of importance.
It might have been specifically designed as a focal point for
traffic. The navigable River Cydnus linked it with the near-by
sea; lively activity prevailed everywhere; merchants from the
most diverse regions of the Roman Empire unloaded their
wares in Tarsus. Every day the youthful Paul was confronted
with what must have been a colourful picture. Is it mere
chance that the world-missionary to-be hailed from a city in
which the widely-travelled merchant was a customary phenomenon? Around Tarsus extended the fertile Cilician plain
protected from the unkind north winds by the snow-covered
peaks of the Taurus mountains. Nevertheless Tarsus was not
cut off from the interior; on the contrary it was actually the
centre of trade between the continent of Asia Minor and the
wide world of the Mediterranean. The road inland led north-
wards over the narrow pass of the "Cilician Gates", which
created the link with western Asia Minor, and thus with Greece
and Rome. To the east the "Syrian Gates" of the Amanus
range offered access to the Oriental-Semitic world. Tarsus lay
therefore at the boundary of two worlds and cultures, destined,
as it were, to be the home of the Apostle to the Nations, who by
his activity was to unite these two worlds anew in Christ.

The history of Tarsus testifies to this encounter between two
worlds. Up to the time of Alexander the Great, Tarsus had
been an Oriental city. Under the rule of the Seleucids it became
exposed to the influence of Hellenism. Antiochus iv (Epiphanes)
against whom in Palestine the Maccabees had waged their
struggle for the Jewish nation, may be regarded as the new
founder of the city. For a time it was called "Antioch-on-

Cydnus" after him, and became a Greek city-state with self-government and the right to its own coinage. Greek prevailed as the common language. Jews did of course settle in Tarsus under Antiochus, a fact that points immediately to the dual character of the city. Its Oriental origins were never wholly to be gainsaid even at the time of greatest Hellenisation. Under Pompey (64 B.C.) Tarsus became the capital of the Roman province of Cilicia. The extending of Roman citizenship to individual inhabitants of the city probably falls in this period. After his assassination Tarsus had to pay dearly for its loyalty to Caesar. Antony came to the aid of the badly stricken city. It was at that time that the Egyptian queen, Cleopatra, dressed as Aphrodite, sailed up the Cydnus towards Mark Antony in a magnificent ship in order to win him by her amorous wiles. Eventually Augustus bestowed his especial favour upon the city. Thereafter it enjoyed firm order and security and a growing prosperity; its population and fame increased apace.

The city's particular pride was its university. Strabo, an historian and geographer at the time of Augustus, did not hesitate to rank it with those of Athens and Alexandria. Even though his judgment may have been exaggerated, it is none-theless a testimony to the standing which the University of Tarsus enjoyed. It was here that the Stoic philosophy flourished, in fact, this philosophy had its home in the south-east corner of Asia Minor. Its ennobling influence upon even the general population astonished many an observer in Augustus's day. In Tarsus one encountered a moral austerity that was unusual in other cities. An example of this austerity was the custom in Tarsus of veiling women. When Paul later forbade the un-veiling of women in the Church at Corinth and justified his decision with the words: "We recognize no other practice" (1 Cor. XI.16), he undoubtedly had in mind the custom of his native city. As a child Saul might well have seen the celebrated Athenodorus (c. 74 B.C.–A.D. 7), Tarsus's most famous philosopher. Athenodorus received his higher education in Tarsus and spent the last twenty years of his life there in a leading capacity. As a former teacher and friend of Augustus he did not hesitate to speak the truth even to the Emperor. After his death the people of Tarsus erected a temple to him and honoured him as a hero at an annual commemoration. We know his philosophy to some extent from fragments in Seneca. His main interest related to ethics. His thinking found expression in noble principles and culminated in the doctrine of conscience: "Know this: you will not be rid of your passions until you have reached the point of asking God for nothing that you could not ask for openly." "Live with men as if God were watching, and speak to God as if men were listening." "Every man's conscience is his god." We can neither ascertain nor presume any direct influence of Athenodorus upon Paul; but that the Apostle had a general acquaintance with this climate of ideas is certain. Paul's frequent references to the "conscience" in his letters must derive from this acquaintance, for the expression was not current in Palestinian Judaism.

The encounter of two worlds in Tarsus, the Hellenistic and the Oriental, is noticeable in the city's religion. The gods of the imperial era certainly had Greek names, but they were essentially Oriental. Religious syncretism prevailed in Tarsus, as it did throughout the Roman Empire. By "syncretism" we mean the mingling and approximation to one another of the religions of the day. Behind the multitude of different gods men sensed the one divine Being. Every race called its gods by other names; but, so it was then held, the different names covered basically the same figures. Thus in the religious sphere we see a process similar to that in the political sphere; the religious interchange between East and West corresponded to their unification at a political level, although in the former case the East was the giving side. Ancient Oriental gods and cults penetrated to the West in a new form and were made to help satisfy its unquenched religious longings. Tarsus offered a picture of this process in miniature, for from ancient times two divinities had been worshipped here before all others. Attempts have been made to epitomise them under the headings of the "sublime" and the "working" gods. The sublime god was portrayed as an Oriental ruler seated upon a mighty throne with a sceptre in his right hand. He bore the name "Baaltars," which means Lord of Tarsus, and was later placed on a level with Zeus. The more he retreated in his sublimity into supra-mundane aloofness the more the "working" god occupied the foreground as his mediator. The name of this god was "Sandon." Under the influence of Hellenism he gradually became identified with Heracles. Pictures depict him standing, but in all other respects he was totally un-Heraclean. Most striking of all is the picture of the god standing upon the funeral pyre. This relates to the Festival of the Funeral Pyre that was celebrated annually in honour of the god, and makes it clear that in Sandon we have a vegetation god such as was also known under other names in Syria, Phrygia, Egypt and Babylon. The fate of the god as portrayed in the Festival of the Funeral Pyre was a symbolic representation of death and resurrection in nature. The myth of the dying and rising god that was widespread throughout the Near East had long been known to Paul, when he found a new meaning and unexpected fulfilment for it in the death and resurrection of Christ.

The veneration of Sandon exemplifies many features which were characteristic of the then widespread mystery-cults. He who desired to undergo initiation had to prepare himself during a probationary period which involved all kinds of privations and trials. When the day of initiation came, the dying and resurrection of the god were carried out symbolically on the person of the devotee himself. When he eventually appeared before the assembled congregation clad in heavenly white robes he was greeted jubilantly by them as though he were the god himself. Through the initiation he had become one with the god and now had a share in his immortal life. In Paul's letters we find many linguistic echoes of the mystery cults. Paul's references to the believer "putting on" Christ undoubtedly derive from conceptions of this kind. By adopting their idiom of speech Paul could hope to make himself understood by those who had formerly been heathen. Again we see the sway of providence, for it is of the greatest significance that Paul, who was to be mistaken for a Greek by the Greeks (cf. 1 Cor. IX.21), should have grown up in a city like Tarsus. One does not need to presume, on that account, any direct influencing of Paul through, say, the cult of Mithras which was indigenous there; the fact suffices that Paul was surrounded by such an atmosphere.

Tarsus was also, however, the seat of a considerable Jewish community. Since the time of King Antiochus Epiphanes (171 B.C.), the Jews in Tarsus had formed a separate exclusive political body, a colony in fact. Many, if not all, possessed the freedom of the city, which could indeed be purchased for gold. Paul himself possessed it (Acts XXI.39). The freedom of the city was a preliminary condition of Roman citizenship, which Paul possessed from birth (Acts XXII.28). We do not know how his father acquired it; perhaps in a similar way to so many Jews of that time. In the year 63 Pompey had brought a great number of captured Jews to the slave market in Rome, but when they were later set free by their Roman masters they received the rights of citizenship. As a Roman citizen Paul was exempt from the punishment of flogging and had the right of appeal to Caesar; both privileges were to acquire significance later in Paul's life. As a Roman citizen he bore from birth the Latin name "Paul"; at home he was called by his Jewish name "Saul," which means, when translated, "asked." The idea that Paul first received the Latin name as a Christian, and that thus from being "Saul" he became "Paul" derives from a misinterpretation of Acts XIII.9. Paul, like so many of the Diaspora, that is, Jews living outside Palestine, had borne a double name from the beginning.

How then are we to picture Paul's early days in Tarsus? The Hellenistic environment must have made an impression upon the alert boy. There was much for him to see as a child that remained for ever denied to the Palestinian Jew. The boy Saul would not have walked blindly through this world, which was magnificent in spite of many symptoms of decadence. The Apostle's imagery, so completely different from that of Jesus, suggests a close acquaintance with the metropolitan life of antiquity. It is from Paul that we hear of the stadium, the race and the prize, of military activities and triumphant processions. We shall not go far wrong if we see in these, too, the influence of youthful impressions. The intellectual and religious life of the city had doubtless aroused many queries in the boy's mind, even though there can be no question of him being really preoccupied with it. He will have listened to so many of the wandering "philosophers," who in street and market-place at that time delivered their discourses upon a reasonable and natural mode of life. At all events, the style of Paul's letters shows signs of having been influenced by the diction of this movement. Above all, however, it is important to bear one thing in mind: the Jew of the Diaspora was linked with his

Hellenistic environment by the Greek language. Paul did not learn Greek laboriously but spoke it from the very beginning. The Jews of the Diaspora even read their Bible in a Greek translation. Yet by nothing is the mind more moulded than by language. Whoever assumes the language of another people receives unconsciously something of the thinking and feeling of that people. That applies to Paul, the citizen of Tarsus and Rome, as well as to the Diaspora Jews in general. A greater susceptibility to all things Roman and Hellenistic was thus a natural characteristic of the Diaspora Jew as opposed to the Palestinian Jew.

That does not in any way mean an absorption into Hellenism. This was prevented, for one thing, by the difference of race, which at that time was keenly felt on both sides. But it was even more their religious exclusiveness which caused the Jews to cling to the inheritance of their fathers. That applies even to a man like the Jewish philosopher Philo, a contemporary of Jesus, whose numerous writings represent the closest possible approach of Judaism to Hellenistic thought. Paul's parental home appears to have been very conservative in religious matters. The fact of merging into a separate political body made it easier for the Jews in Tarsus to preserve their individuality. In Romans XVI, 7 and 11, Paul sends greetings to Andronicus, Junias and Herodion, his "kinsmen"; we may accordingly presume that they belonged with him to the Jewish national association in Tarsus. It is doubtful whether Paul attended a non-Jewish school as a boy, and received a Greek education at first hand, but it is certain that his home upbringing was determined by the Jewish tradition. The Apostle still boasted proudly of his Jewish descent: "Circumcised on the eighth day, of the people of Israel, of the tribe of Benjamin, a Hebrew born of Hebrews" (Phil. III.5). Biblical instruction began for the boy at the age of five. He learned the main contents of the Law (Deut. V and VI), and steeped himself in the history of his people. The patriarchs were without any doubt more real in his imagination than the great figures of Greek and Roman history. The primeval tradition of his people was surrounded for him by the aura of sanctity and must have filled him with pride. The hope of the promised Messiah to come made his heart beat faster. This Messiah was to subject the whole world to the God of Israel. The boy could not as yet suspect how very differently this promise would achieve fulfilment, and that he would one day be called upon to devote his life to the true Messiah.

A new chapter in his education began at the age of ten. The boy was now made familiar with the "oral" Law. The doctors of the Law had drawn up innumerable regulations in exposition of the Law; and the study of these now became a duty. As soon as Paul began to emerge from boyhood he was obliged to shoulder the whole of the Law; the age for this was later fixed at thirteen. From all sides it was now drummed into the boy: "Thou shalt not! Thou shalt not!" The scribes had deduced six hundred and thirteen commandments from the Old Testament Law. The fact that the prohibitions (365) outnumbered the positive precepts (248) is indicative of the spirit of this legal instruction. The fear of error was stronger than the joy of obedience; something oppressive lay over the life of this legally devout boy. How easy it was to offend against one of these commandments! Who could ever keep all of them constantly in mind? To be sure, the Law was also Israel's pride and joy. Even Paul, for whom Christ was "the end of the law" (Rom. x.4), still found words to say in praise of the Law: "The law is holy, and the commandment is holy and just and good" (Rom. vii.12).

His assumption of the Law at that time must certainly have caused a painful break in his development. The impressive description that Paul gives in Rom. vii of the dichotomy in the human heart may well go back to this experience of his youth. "If it had not been for the law, I should not have known sin. I should not have known what it is to covet if the law had not said, 'You shall not covet.' But sin, finding opportunity in the commandment, wrought in me all kinds of covetousness. Apart from the law sin lies dead. I was once alive apart from the law, but when the commandment came, sin revived and I died" (Rom. vii.7ff.) Of course, we are not dealing, in this description, with a purely private experience that Paul had in his youth. Paul's words go far beyond the narrow bounds of a personal experience, and reproduce the experience of the non-Christian as it is seen in the light of Christ. Nevertheless, the fact that Paul can describe this experience so personally and so vividly reveals that he himself has undergone it. This does not mean that we have to think of any particular sin in the life of the youthful Paul. Perhaps it was only when he looked back as a Christian that he realised what had happened within him when he was "born under the law" (Gal. iv.4). But we can understand from this the jubilation of the Apostle, whom Christ had delivered from slavery to the Law.

Of course at that time Paul stood only at the beginning of the road upon which he was to be found "as to righteousness under the law blameless" (Phil. iii.6). Perhaps it was an already understood thing that, when he grew up, he should proceed to the high school for Scribes and Pharisees in Jerusalem. Connexions with Jerusalem existed quite apart from this. Pilgrimages to the Temple were no rarity for Jews of the Diaspora. Many a Jew was drawn in the evening of his life to the land of his fathers. We also know of a sister of Paul whose son was later in Jerusalem (Acts xxiii.16). The scribes of that day had to practise their profession free of charge, and most of them learned a trade besides. Paul himself was trained in such a trade; and later, on his missionary journeys, it was to prove very useful to him. Paul learned tent-making, presumably in his father's workshop in Tarsus. The famous Cilician goat-hair must have provided the raw material for this trade.

So Paul grew up in the city in which two worlds met and mingled. His own life is a reflection of this process in miniature. The eastward march of Alexander the Great had brought these two worlds close to each other. The boy from Tarsus was destined to begin a march of triumph in the opposite direction. Certainly he did not do this on his own authority, and he was not concerned with the union of East and West; those whom Paul brought together found themselves in a higher unity, in the fellowship of members in the body of which Christ is the Head.

# JERUSALEM

JERUSALEM was for the Jews of those days the holy city *par excellence*. The whole life of this city was dominated by religious conceptions and associated with religion; in fact, this city owed her importance in the main to religion, of which she had become, in a special sense, a shrine. Even today, long after the Jewish Temple has ceased to be a focal centre, Jerusalem is still the city of religion. She has become the holy city for Christians and Mohammedans also, and her history to the present day is bound up with this fact. To be sure, where today we see the co-existence of violently contrasting religious customs and conceptions, at that time there reigned the strictest uniformity in basic principles, in spite of every diversity of practice. In her centuries-long history Jerusalem had become the centre of the Jewish religion and thus of Judaism as a whole. As regards its natural situation, Jerusalem was a hill city, poor in water, whose position from the point of view of commerce and traffic was not at all favourable. Yet since the time of David (*c.* 1000 B.C.) Jerusalem had become the political and then, in increasing measure, the religious, centre of Judaism. This has to do above all with the centralisation of worship. From the time of Jeremiah (*c.* 600 B.C.) onwards the regulations of the Book of Deuteronomy had been in force, according to which sacrifices were to be offered at no shrine other than the Temple at Jerusalem. This was a drastic reform of great severity, necessary, however, on account of the threatened mingling with heathen practices. What the country as a whole thereby lost, the capital city gained; she became the religious centre. This was even more so in the post-exilic period, when the people had made their way back from Babylonian captivity. The Jewish monarchy was dead; the political role of Jerusalem had been played out. All the more emphasis was placed, therefore, on the religious significance of the city. Jerusalem became the holy city, just as Rome did in the Middle Ages.

The symbol of this "holiness," visible from far and wide, was still, in Jesus's day, the Temple. No longer was it Solomon's

Temple, nor even the post-exilic structure that had replaced it. The Roman puppet king Herod (Mt. ii.1ff.), who was keen on building, had commissioned, in the eighteenth year of his reign (20-19 B.C.), a magnificent new Temple for the Jews; it was not completed until A.D. 63. On Mount Zion, where the Temple formerly stood, the new Temple area was laid out in a rectangle, 375 yards wide and 600 yards long, and surrounded by mighty walls. Colonnades adjoined the walls the whole way round, and in them were situated the synagogue rooms (Lk. ii.46ff.), where the Rabbis delivered their lectures to their pupils and where also the Christians later held their first gatherings (Acts ii.1ff., iii.11, v.12). Through the colonnades one had access to the outer court, which was usually described as the Court of Gentiles. It was open to all, Jews and Gentiles alike, and it was here that the merchants and money-changers set up their stalls (Jn. ii.14ff.) The sacred buildings were hidden from the public gaze by strong walls. Warning notices forbade every non-Jew, on pain of death, to set foot in the holy place (Acts xxi.27ff.) Through the Court of Women and the Court of the Israelites one came to the Court of Priests with the gigantic altar of burnt offering. The Temple-house itself consisted, as far as we know, of the Porch, the Holy Place and the Holy of Holies. In the Holy Place stood the seven-branched lampstand, the table with the shewbread and the altar of incense. The Holy of Holies, which the High Priest was only permitted to enter once a year, was empty; only a low stone stood in place of the Ark of the Covenant.

The Herodian Temple was not a first-class work of art; it achieved its effect much more by its sheer weight and splendour. Seen from the Mount of Olives especially, it must have made a wonderful impression upon the onlooker. When the whole area was bathed in sunlight it sparkled and gleamed with gold and marble, and many a person must have cried out with the disciples: "Look, Teacher, what wonderful stones and what wonderful buildings!" (Mk. xiii.1).

As the city in which the Temple stood, the only place where a valid sacrifice could be offered to the Lord, Jerusalem exercised an indescribable fascination upon the Jewish world of that time. Jerusalem was the place of God's presence upon earth. Moreover, care was taken by means of legal regulations to see that

Jerusalem was not forgotten. Every male adult had to appear
three times a year in Jerusalem at the three main festivals.
Practice, it is true, does not appear to have corresponded
wholly with these precepts. Those who lived further away
undertook the journey only once a year, we gather, and that at
the Feast of the Passover (Lk. ii.41). The women would
frequently have accompanied their husbands, though they were
not obliged to do so. Boys of twelve years of age were generally
no longer regarded as minors. It is doubtful whether the Jews
of the Diaspora undertook the journey even once a year. Perhaps they contented themselves with one journey in a lifetime.
But even with these reservations the influx of festival pilgrims
meant a great deal to Jerusalem and left its mark upon the
city: "Jerusalem, built as a city which is bound firmly together,
to which the tribes go up, the tribes of the Lord, as was decreed
for Israel, to give thanks to the name of the Lord" (Ps. cxxii.3
and 4). According to recent estimates the population at the
time of Jesus totalled about fifty-five thousand; the number of
festival pilgrims has been assessed at a hundred and twenty-five
thousand.

Wherever there is sacrifice, there is the priest. Jerusalem,
as the city of the Temple, was also the chief seat of the priesthood, which formed the main part of the upper social layer of
that time. At the head of the whole priesthood stood the High
Priest, who was regarded as God's plenipotentiary, and thus
had to make the expiatory sacrifice for the people at the great
Feast of the Atonement. By virtue of his exceptional position
in the cult he was invested with the highest dignity, and was
therefore the first representative of his people in the political
sphere also. He had as his aides the chief priests, priests and
Levites. The ordinary priesthood, whose homes were scattered
all over Judaea and Galilee, was divided into twenty-four
priestly divisions, which were summoned to conduct Temple
worship in turns (Lk. 1.5, 8f.) The Levites formed the minor
clergy who were responsible for the performing of the Temple
music and the conduct of the minor Temple services. The total
Jewish priesthood of Jesus's day has been estimated as at least
eighteen thousand priests and Levites.

But Jerusalem was not only the city of the noisy Temple
feasts, but also the seat of the Academy of Law. It was un-

doubtedly this, above all, that drew the young Paul to this city. There were two groups who had in special measure set themselves the task of cultivating the Law: the Scribes and the Pharisees; and Paul entered into the closest relationship with both. By Jesus's day both groups had, in addition to the already existing upper class of priests, won for themselves an increasingly distinguished social position and a high regard among the people.

The more the Jewish religion became in the post-exilic era a religion of the Book, the greater necessity there was for a special class that would occupy itself fully with the sacred Book of this religion. The Hebrew in which the Old Testament was, with some small exceptions, written, was no longer immediately intelligible to the Jews of that time; in Palestine in Jesus's day Aramaic, a west-Semitic dialect, was spoken. Thus, from the purely linguistic angle, a certain erudition was necessary for the understanding of the Old Testament. But, beyond that, the scribes felt themselves called upon to expound in lectures the Old Testament, which was for them chiefly a book of law, to discuss it in hair-splitting detail, and to deduce from it rules and principles of law for both public and private life. They were therefore at the same time theologians and lawyers. As such they enjoyed the highest esteem of the people, although they came partly from the lowest classes. They allowed themselves to be addressed as "Rabbi" or "Father" (Mt. xxiii.7, 9); they occupied places of honour at table or in the synagogue, and were greeted respectfully by all the people, who recognised them by their long robes. Their power rested upon their knowledge. Only after years of study was a man received into their fraternity, in return for which they held in their hands the leading positions in the administration of justice, government and education. They also had the right to become members of the highest authority, the council of seventy-one, the so-called Sanhedrin. Only recently has another fact been recognised, which enables us to understand the high regard accorded to the scribes; they were, in addition to all this, the custodians of the secret lore, the esoteric tradition, which was invested with a divine lustre. They busied themselves with teachings concerning the mysteries of God's Being, with pronouncements about the heavenly and subterranean worlds, and

c

also, above all, with views concerning the last things, in other words with the so-called "Apocalyptic." The conception of the "Son of Man," which in turn plays such a great role in the New Testament, also belonged to the apocalyptic teachings. These secret doctrines, which were set down in various writings, were regarded as divinely inspired. But even the oral tradition, and indeed the text of the Bible itself, were not rendered immediately accessible to the masses. In the first century after Christ there were scribes who, on these grounds, rejected the Aramaic translations of the Old Testament, the so-called *Targums*. By virtue of their secret lore the scribes were deemed successors of the prophets. Only this fact explains fully why they enjoyed such respect in spite of their proud contempt for the "people." Their tombs were honoured, next to those of the patriarchs and prophets, as the tombs of saints.

The Pharisees must be carefully distinguished from the Scribes; in fact, their title means "the separated ones." It was they who advanced the claim that they were the true congregation of Israel. We are here dealing with closed communities with rigid terms of admission. Those who belonged to them assumed special obligations relating to the discharge of the Law. These consisted largely in purity-regulations and the payment of tithes. The Pharisees' pride was founded upon such works of supererogation (Lk. xviii.12). Scribes were also numbered among the Pharisees; but the two groups must not on that account be equated. Even priests were to be found among the Pharisees; but above all their communities comprised men of the people, merchants, tradesmen, farmers, all men without any scribal education. Like the scribes, these also were generally held in high regard by the people on account of their strict adherence to the Law, though at the time of Jesus there were not lacking also those who "laboured and were heavy laden," who sighed under their harsh yoke. The New Testament picture of the Pharisee, which has led to his becoming the proverbial hypocrite, is one-sided and only to be understood as part of Jesus's polemic against this group. Certainly Jesus perceived and ruthlessly exposed the weak point in their piety. But, for all that, we must not overlook the unexampled earnestness with which these men sought to submit their whole life, down to the smallest detail, to the Law of God, and which procured for them the respectful admiration of the people.

That was the world, therefore, into which the young Paul, possibly fifteen years old, now entered, and which he greedily assimilated. We must now look at its intellectual and religious outlook a little more closely.

From the Acts of the Apostles (XXII.3) we learn that Paul sat "at the feet" of the famous Rabbi Gamaliel. There is no reason to throw doubt upon this statement; it is to be taken quite literally. We must picture the pursuit of studies in the rabbinic academy at Jerusalem in similar terms to that in the present-day stronghold of Islamic studies, the university mosque of El Azhar in Cairo. The teacher lectured from a raised seat; around him on the floor sat the pupils. We must completely dismiss the idea of a lecture room. But even the lecturing and the study do not compare with our academic standards. There was no question of free investigation. The object was rather to learn by heart the opinions of the various authorities in order eventually to swear by the words of one's own master. At the centre of all instruction stood the Old Testament. The pupil had, of course, to commit it extensively to memory, but that in itself was not sufficient. In addition he had to impress upon his memory the oral tradition, that is, the most important expositions of the famous rabbis. This tradition was called the *Mishna*, *i.e.* "teaching" (literally "repetition"). It was treated as secret, and could not therefore be taken down, but had to be retained in the memory without notes. In the light of this we can understand the rabbinic saying: "A scholar must be like a well encrusted with lime that loses not a drop." Two kinds of scripture study were pursued: the *Haggada* and the *Halakha*. The *Haggada* concerned itself mainly with a free elaboration of the historical narratives of the Old Testament. Thus innumerable things, some of a truly absurd nature, were read into the Creation story. The lives of the patriarchs offered a rich opportunity for fantastic embellishment, especially the story of Moses. We have an example of this kind of historical *Midrash* (exposition of Scripture) in the speech of Stephen (Acts VII). Paul also shows himself familiar with the *Haggada*: a water-dispensing rock accompanied the Israelites throughout their journey in the wilderness (1 Cor. x.4); the Law was given to Moses not by God Himself, but through the mediation of angels (Gal. III.19; cf. Acts VII.53, Heb. II.2); in II Tim. III.8, the Egyptian magicians who withstood Moses and Aaron are named.

Besides the filling out of the Old Testament narratives by the unfettered imagination we find allegorical interpretation, or re-interpretation. This also is used by Paul on occasions. Thus he interprets the accompanying rock to mean Christ (I Cor. x.4), and the maid Hagar to mean the covenant on Sinai (Gal. IV.24). Underlying the allegorical interpretation is the view that everything in Scripture must have a deeper spiritual meaning. For that reason Paul relates the humane precept in Deuteronomy XXV.4, "You shall not muzzle an ox when it is treading out the grain" to the preacher, who is worthy of his hire (I Cor. IX.9).

But he would also have adopted the other kind of Scripture study: the *Halakha*. The *Halakha* had to do with the legal passages in the Old Testament. The scribes considered it their task to find a commandment to regulate action in every situation of practical life. To that end they elaborated the Old Testament commandments, reduced them to precepts of even more minute detail, and twisted and turned them until they met practical demands. We call such thinking "casuistry," because it lays down a rule for every case (Latin *casus*) that might arise in daily life, and leaves nothing to the personal freedom and the conscience of the individual. In spite of this treatment of Scripture, the commandments of the Old Testament did not suffice; here, then, as in the *Haggada*, they proceeded to supplement them liberally. As a result there was built up, in addition to the Old Testament law, the *Torah*, a comprehensive common law sustained by the authority of distinguished rabbis. In Paul's day, these scribal additions (Mt. xv.3ff.) were merely passed on orally. Only in the second century after Christ was a start made in writing them down; hence arose the *Talmud*. The precepts of this common law related mainly to the sacrifices, the celebration of the sacred seasons, especially of the Sabbath, the payment of dues to the Temple and the priests, and the statutes regarding purity and impurity. In addition there arose the development of a criminal and civil law, and particularly of the marriage law. The scribes were indeed not only the theologians but also the lawyers of Judaism.

The best-known example of the petty spirit that, for the most part, pervades these precepts, are the commandments relating to the Sabbath. Out of the simple Old Testament command to rest on the Sabbath they ingeniously manufactured a whole host of detailed prohibitions. These were classified into thirty-nine principal categories of work that were forbidden on the Sabbath. But this was only the starting-point for an even pettier casuistry. Reaping, for example, figured among the prohibited labours. But even the plucking of ears of corn was classed as reaping, which is why the disciples were reproached for desecrating the Sabbath (Mt. xii.1f.) Warm food had to be prepared before the onset of the Sabbath, when it might be kept warm artificially, though rigid care had to be taken lest the warmth already present was increased in the process. For that reason, the rabbis prescribed the materials in which food might or might not be stored:

"We may not place (it) in peat, foliage, salt, lime, or sand, whether moist or dry; nor in straw, grapeskins, soft flocking or herbage, when they are moist; but we may store (food) in them when they are dry."

"We may store (food) in garments, produce, dove's wings, carpenters' sawdust and thoroughly beaten hatchelled flax. Rabbi Judah forbids (storing) it in fine, but permits it in coarse (beaten flax)."[1] On the Sabbath one might not climb a tree, ride an animal or slap one's thighs. One might not travel further than 2,000 cubits (*i.e.* 1,000 yards) from one's place of residence. This distance was therefore called a "Sabbath day's journey" (Acts 1.12). If, on the other hand, one deposited at the furthest limit of this distance, before the dawn of the Sabbath, enough food for two meals, one might proceed for another 2,000 cubits, that point being then regarded, as it were, as another place of residence. It was also sufficient merely to designate a tree or stone on the route as a Sabbath resting-place, only this had to be done quite precisely; a vague indication of the spot was insufficient. Two famous scribes argued whether one might eat an egg laid on the Sabbath. When we picture these stipulations to ourselves— and there was no end to them—we can weigh the significance

[1] *The Babylonian Talmud, Seder Moed,* Tractate *"Shabbath,"* tr. H. Freedman, London 1938, vol. i, pp. 217 and 221.

of Jesus's words: "The sabbath was made for man, not man for the sabbath" (Mk. II.27). The purity-regulations, of which the Gospels give us a vivid picture, were similarly minute and petty (cf. Mt. xv.2, xxiii.25-26, Mk. vii.2-5, Lk. xi.38-39).

The aim of these precepts was to subject all life to the Law, in return for which one counted upon the divine recompense. All activity followed the pattern of obedience and reward. The legalism of this piety resulted in the moral life being viewed wholly from the standpoint of the Law. Moral teaching became jurisprudence, and the fact that moral behaviour cannot be submitted to the decrees of formal justice was at the same time overlooked. Piety was of necessity judged by outward behaviour, not by the inner motive; hence, once again, the superficiality of this piety together with the hypocrisy of which Jesus accused it. Thus it could arise that a man might live blamelessly according to the Law, and yet at the same time leave out of account the main thing, love for God and for his neighbour which are the fulfilment of the Law (Mt. xxii.37ff.) A further indication of the superficiality of this piety is the fact that really only the scribe could be pious, for only he knew the countless regulations which it was essential to observe. It was with justice that a celebrated teacher said: "An ignorant man cannot be truly pious," which leads us to understand why a young man like Paul applied himself to the study of scriptural learning. We can also judge from that what a painful break (Phil. iii.7) it was in his life when, in the power of Christ, he tore himself away from all these traditions and, at the peak of his career, delivered the judgment which sums up both the greatness and the weakness of this piety: "They have a zeal for God, but it is not enlightened" (Rom. x.2).

# STEPHEN

ALTHOUGH we can picture the intellectual world into which
Paul entered in connexion with his higher education in
Jerusalem, we know little about his outward fortunes at
this time. We have no information as to how long he attended
the rabbinic academy in Jerusalem and where he stayed after
that. We have not necessarily to think of a return to Tarsus.
It is highly likely that he remained in Jerusalem, the seat of
scribal learning, until we meet him there as a persecutor of the
Christians and opponent of Stephen. His time will have been
taken up mainly with the completion of his law studies, and
with his zealous preoccupation with the traditions of the Fathers.
One question does agitate us: did Paul ever become acquainted
with Jesus? From a purely chronological point of view that
would have been perfectly possible. But there is, unfortunately,
no indication to that effect. It is hardly probable that Paul
would have remained silent about it in his letters. He would
have had occasion to speak about it in connexion with the
various attacks upon his apostolic office. In any event the much
debated passage, II Cor. v.16: "Even though we have known
Christ after the flesh, yet now we know him so no more" (R.V.),
gives us no cause for presupposing Paul's acquaintance with the
earthly Christ. It is not even certain that the "we" of this
statement can be limited to the person of Paul. Moreover the
Greek word for "know" stands for more than a fleeting seeing
and hearing; and there would probably have been even less
question of a "knowing" of this kind. Yet, as we have said,
we cannot go beyond speculations in this matter. Even if Paul
were to have known the Lord in His earthly manifestation, it
had no influence upon his development. Only before Damascus
did he have a decisive encounter with Christ.

Information about Paul occurs for the first time in relation to
the stoning of Stephen (Acts VI, VII). In order to understand
the significance of this story, a short review of the conditions
obtaining in the primitive Church in Jerusalem (Acts I-v) is
necessary.

The primitive Church originated at Pentecost (Acts II); the festival of the Spirit is likewise the birthday of the Church. When the Lord imparted Himself in the Spirit to His disciples as the One who lived, they could not forbear to speak "the things they had seen and heard" (cf. Acts IV.20). Peter's Whitsun sermon created the first Christian community. The primitive Church had not as yet become conscious of the fact that with them something completely new had arisen. Its members considered themselves then as ever to be pious Jews. They took part as usual in the Temple services (Acts III 1, V.12), and observed the Law of the Fathers. In one respect only did they regard themselves as superior to their compatriots and fellow-believers: they knew that the Messiah, for whom Israel had hoped and whom the prophets had foretold, had already appeared. God had made Him, whom the Jews had rejected, and nailed to the Cross, both Messiah (Greek: *Christos*) and Lord (Acts II.36), and this Christ would return in glory (Acts III.20f.) He would not delay much longer, and woe to those who did not use the intervening period for repentance, for a radical conversion and change of heart (Acts II.38, III.17ff., IV.11f., V.30f.) To turn "all the house of Israel" (Acts II.36) to its Messiah and Lord—such was the aim of the Church, which considered itself the true Israel of the final dispensation. The hope of Christ's return animated their gatherings, where, in solemn table fellowship at the Lord's Table, they revived the memory of the departed Lord, and experienced with joyful hearts the presence of the exalted One; this same hope led to the blossoming of a springtime of first love, in which the fellowship of the faith became a genuine brotherhood (Acts II.44-47).

With Stephen and his followers a new element entered the primitive Church. Stephen belonged to the seven almoners who were ordained by the apostles for the better maintenance of the Church (Acts VI.1f.) Acts describes him as a man "full of faith and of the Holy Spirit" (Acts VI.5) by whose hand "great wonders and signs" had been done among the people (Acts VI.8). One thing above all is important for an understanding of his appearance upon the scene: Stephen was not a Palestinian, but a Diaspora Jew. In Acts the Diaspora Jews are called "Hellenists" on account of their language. Stephen was one of their number, as is suggested by his Greek name, which means "crown" or "garland," a name that appears so thoroughly appropriate for the first martyr of the Christian Church. To be sure, the Greek name is still no proof that he originated from the Diaspora; we know of Palestinian Jews in this period with Greek names. More information can be gleaned from the statement that Stephen appeared in the synagogue of the Diaspora Jews in Jerusalem (Acts VI.9). We see from this that there was a whole crowd of Diaspora Jews who had become resident in Jerusalem. By the "freedmen" presumably we must understand the descendants of the Jews who came to Rome under Pompey as prisoners-of-war, and were then set free by their masters.

In many respects the Diaspora Jews had a freer and more progressive attitude than those of their fellow-believers who had remained in Palestine. For all their strict adherence to the religion of their fathers, they could not and would not withdraw themselves from the influence of the Graeco-Roman world. As only the one Temple existed—and that in Jerusalem—their worship was of necessity without sacrifice or priesthood. The synagogue service consisted only of preaching and prayer. To many educated heathen Judaism appeared on that account to be a "philosophical" religion. As public life was in no way subject to the Jewish Law, the Jews of the Diaspora adopted in many matters a freer attitude towards the Law. It was no coincidence, probably, that both these points—the attitude towards worship and the Law—played a part in the trial of Stephen (Acts VI.13). They are here, of course, linked up with his proclamation of Christ (Acts VI.14). But why is the same objection not raised against the preaching of Christ by Peter and the first apostles (cf. Acts IV.13-17, V.28)? Clearly because in that instance it would have been irrelevant. The first apostles did not wish to overstep the bounds of Judaism with their witness to Christ. In spite of all the turbulence that had entered their lives through the influence of Jesus, they were men of simple conservative mind. Not so with Stephen! His descent from Diaspora Judaism asserted itself in his preaching of Christ. His spirit was boldly directed forwards. The first apostles saw in Christ the fulfilment of the old Covenant. Stephen sensed the revolutionary character of Jesus's preaching. Jesus had in fact changed the "customs which Moses delivered"

(Acts vi.14). Of course Jesus knew, as far as we can gather, that He was the first to have brought out the real meaning of the Old Testament Law (Mt. v.17, 21ff., 27ff., 33ff., 38ff., 43ff., XXII.34ff.); but as a result He had deliberately offended the legalistic piety of His contemporaries by, for instance, His infringement of the Sabbath regulations. Jesus's views on purity and impurity (Mk. vii.14f.) signify, fundamentally, an abrogation of the legal system. Side by side in Jesus's attitude to the Law there run a conservative and a revolutionary strand. The first apostles held to the former; Stephen appreciated the latter. Thus one count of the charge against him was certainly not a simple fabrication. The other count, which speaks of the destruction of the Temple, is presumably the distorted form of a pronouncement that goes back to Jesus Himself (Mk. xiii.2). Perhaps Stephen held it out in his polemic as a threat against the Jews, self-assured and proud of their sanctuary. But even on this point the attitude of the Diaspora Jews, who could, at a pinch, conceive of religion without even a centre of worship, may have played a part. Indeed, in Stephen's speech before the Sanhedrin, Solomon's erection of the Temple is represented as actually a misunderstanding of God's will (Acts vii.47f.) Views are here expressed which in many respects recall the scene in John's Gospel, where Jesus sits opposite a Samaritan woman and speaks to her of the worship of God in spirit and truth.

In the Greek world Stephen would have aroused no disapproval with utterances of this kind. When Paul expressed similar thoughts on the Areopagus (Acts xvii.24ff. see pp. 83ff.) the Athenians listened calmly. Here in Jerusalem they were destined to encounter the most violent opposition. Stephen was dragged before the highest Jewish authority. Wild charges were hurled against him. His defence was drowned amidst the tumult of the fanatical mob.[1] Was the whole thing a regular judicial process, or are we dealing here with a case of "lynch law"? It is now too late to find out exactly what happened. Sufficient to note that they thrust him out of the city, and that, amidst

---

[1] One cannot assume that Stephen actually delivered at this moment the long, learned and calm speech recorded in Acts vii. With the exception of the closing vss. (51-53) it is rather a model example of a Midrash (Jewish scriptural exposition). It may on that account contain ideas such as Stephen presented on other occasions in the synagogue.

the stone throwing of the witnesses, the first martyr of the
Christian Church commended his spirit into Jesus's hands.

It is at this point that Paul (Saul) emerges for the first time
in the Acts' account (Acts vii.58). According to the description
as a whole he appears to have taken a prominent part in the
trial of Stephen. The detail given to the effect that the witnesses
laid their garments at Saul's feet does not, of course, immediately justify this assumption. Perhaps this was only intended to fit Paul into the narrative. But because Paul appears
afterwards as a particularly zealous persecutor (Acts viii.3),
and because he was entrusted with a special mission (Acts ix)
in this matter by the Supreme Council, we may well attribute
importance to this small detail of the narrative. In the light of
Paul's temperament (cf. ii Cor. xi.29) we may easily believe that
he sided passionately in the affair. Probably they had already
observed potential qualities of leadership in the "young man,"
as Saul is here described (Acts vii.58)—we must imagine him
therefore to be about thirty years old. We shall not go far
wrong then if we ascribe the supervision of the execution to Saul.
His willing participation in this terrible event and his assent to
it is at any rate explicitly confirmed (Acts viii.1).

How is it possible that Paul should have taken this step, and
indeed that his fanaticism was far from being quenched even
then? We know the spirit to which Paul had committed himself in his Jerusalem period. Paul had become both scribe and
Pharisee (Acts xxvi.5, Phil. iii.5). With this mentality he had
encountered the Christians in Jerusalem, and had collided
above all with Stephen. The passionate disciple of the rabbis
may well have been amongst the people of the synagogue of
the Cilicians who disputed and wrangled with Stephen. He
had probably also opposed Stephen in debate personally. The
assertion that the crucified Jesus was the promised Messiah of
Israel would have called forth his burning protest. It was the
scribe in him that was aroused in opposition. How could a
crucified man be the anointed of God? It was even written:
"A hanged man is accursed by God" (Deut. xxi.23). God
Himself had pronounced His verdict upon this Nazarene; His
disciples were following a fatal will-o'-the-wisp and were
setting themselves up against the sacred revelation of God.
Such would have been the judgment of Paul the scribe. We

can infer this from a later utterance of the Apostle (Gal. III.13)
—a real piece of rabbinic logic, and of human thinking as well.
The pagan Celsus, who was the first to direct a comprehensive
attack upon Christianity in the middle of the second century,
judged no differently. That God should have led His Envoy
upon earth along this path, that He should have allowed Him
to die in disgrace and shame between two criminals, and that
His work was as good as shipwrecked in His death, remained to
all unenlightened eyes a "stumbling-block" and "folly"
(1 Cor. 1.23), and, even for a Christian, lay hidden in the depths
of God's inscrutable wisdom. In truth, we understand only too
well why Paul the scribe resisted this insight with all the re-
sources of his scholastic theology. Moreover, what the Christians further related concerning the Resurrection of this crucified
Man and His Ascension, must have seemed a silly fairy-tale to
him. What weight did the dreams of uneducated fishermen
and stupid women carry with him? Why had this crucified
One not appeared to any of the learned men of Israel? "Have
any of the authorities or of the Pharisees believed in him? But
this crowd, who do not know the law, are accursed" (Jn.
VII.48f.)

Not only the learning of the scribe but also the pride of the
Pharisee in Paul rebelled against this Jesus of Nazareth. The
great power in the life of Israel was the Law, which the Pharisee
served with heart and soul. To impugn the Law was to touch
the most sacred thing that existed, an action worthy of death.
But what were they now saying of this Galilean? He had pronounced His woes upon the Pharisees and the scribes (Mt.
XXIII), and sat at table with tax-gatherers and sinners (Mt. IX.11).
He had uttered the unheard-of blasphemy: God loves the one
sinner who repents more than the ninety-nine righteous, who
need no repentance (Lk. xv.7). He had wantonly disregarded
the Sabbath rules and exempted His disciples from fasting
(Mk. II.18ff.) He had set up the unclean Samaritan as an example to the Jew (Lk. x.30ff., XVII.11ff.) He had declared the
righteous God of Israel to be arbitrary (Mt. xx.1-16). Yes,
Stephen was certainly right: "He will change the customs
which Moses delivered to us." What was the outcome to be?
If the Law was no longer valid, it meant the ruin of Israel. A
fearful judgment of God threatened if the people did not try all

possible means of averting this evil. And if blood had to flow in the process—"Cursed is he who does the work of the Lord with slackness; and cursed is he who keeps back his sword from bloodshed" (Jer. XLVIII.10). Paul the Pharisee thus became the fanatical persecutor of the Christians. Again we must point out the genuine Pharisaism of this—and yet, is this attitude so remote from men of all ages and races? Is not the message that God stoops to the sinner and overlooks the proud and self-righteous, foolish even for the twentieth-century Aryan? Does not the latter also appeal to God's justice and, with sure confidence in his own achievement, gladly renounce the free gift of grace? Does not modern man also conceive the moral world-order in exactly the same terms as the law-abiding Pharisee, and must he not likewise regard Jesus, the Saviour of sinners, as a disturbing intruder into this sacred realm? Even our pagan Celsus would have cause to utter his powerful aphorism again. No, we do not wish to wrong Paul the Pharisee; we understand him even though perhaps we cannot muster the same fanaticism for the "just cause."

Again, this fanaticism may possibly have a psychological explanation. Two observations help us here. The one relates to Gamaliel, Paul's tutor. All that is handed down to us regarding him are merely a few legal pronouncements, which hardly give any indication of his religious disposition. That he later became a Christian is legend. However, Acts does give us some information about his attitude to the trials of the Christians in Jerusalem, the historicity of which we have no firm grounds for disputing (Acts v.34-39). According to this information Gamaliel counselled leniency and caution because there was doubt as to whether this cause was of God or not. This waiting attitude of his hitherto highly-honoured teacher may have been a bitter disappointment to the perfervid scholar. His confidence in him received a blow from which it was never to recover. What sort of danger did this sect of the Nazarenes represent if even this master in Israel could become hesitant! At this point Paul felt the weight of responsibility resting upon his shoulders. If the elders no longer discerned the signs of the times, it was up to their juniors to take the initiative. Thus it may have been precisely the wise restraint of his old teacher which fanned the flames of fanaticism in Paul. We know nothing of this, because we have absolutely no information on the point; but we can assume this much from what we know of the psychological behaviour of individuals.

A second attempt at a psychological explanation of young Saul's fanaticism is linked with a phrase in the conversion narrative. In one of the three accounts of Paul's conversion (see p. 40), we find the sentence: "It hurts you to kick against the goads" (Acts xxvi.14). Underlying this proverbial expression is the image of the stick, furnished at one end with a goad used to drive the ox when ploughing. May we gather something from this phrase? We must note, first of all, that it occurs in only one of the three accounts. It does not belong, therefore, to the unanimous section of the tradition. Thus, at a pinch, it might refer to the Apostle's future; meaning that he would no longer be able to evade the urgings of Christ. But its connexion with the preceding words ("why do you persecute me?") makes it more likely to refer to Saul's previous development. The figure of Christ must already have made an impression upon Saul the Pharisee and scribe: but he must have recoiled from this influence. It is indeed quite conceivable that, for instance, the spirit of brotherly love which animated the primitive Church in Jerusalem gave him cause to think: could a faith which transformed life in this manner really be so mistaken? It is similarly improbable that a man like Paul who, as his letters show, was capable of the tenderest feelings, despite his violent nature, could have remained absolutely unmoved at the sight of the dying Stephen, even though he did have some hand in the man's death. The steadfastness and religious submission with which Stephen went to his death cannot have failed to make some impression upon him. The question would have arisen in his mind: can the Master, whose disciples die like this for Him, really be a will-o'-the-wisp? But he suppresses this doubt within himself, and kills it as he surrenders himself fully at last to his persecuting zeal. The psychological law which becomes apparent here is well known. How many a man seeks to hide his inner uncertainty behind some particularly zealous deed! How frequently must decisive action serve to allay inward doubt! How often must fanaticism take the place of inner clarity which is lacking! We talk here of a "compensation of feelings." Might not this psychological law perhaps have come into operation in Saul's case? We do not know for sure; but at least it is not improbable. Possibly Paul had already undergone, as a Pharisee, that experience of the Law which he later described in opposition to Peter (Gal. II.15f.) The vivid description in Rom. VII (see pp. 134ff.) would accord with this. Thus it was perhaps a last desperate protest against the collapse of his traditional world-view that made Paul become the fanatical persecutor of the Christians.

Today we can discern the hand of God in Paul's following of this road. Just as Luther without his "monkery" could not have overcome Catholicism from within, in the same way Paul had to exhaust the last and deepest possibilities of Judaism, in order to proclaim the unlegalistic Gospel of the Gentiles. The more painful the break, the deeper it goes. Only he who has been bound can experience freedom. Paul freed Christianity from the limitations of Judaism; that was the world mission of one who had been wholly a Jew. The Pharisee was the forerunner of the Apostle.

# DAMASCUS

B UT that the Pharisee became the apostle was due not to his
"will" or "exertion," but to God's mercy (Rom. ix.16).
This word, written later by Paul out of his own life-
experience, applies also to what is called his "Damascus experience."

Paul had exercised his persecuting zeal first of all upon the
Church in Jerusalem (Acts viii.3). Certainly in this case it did
not develop into such an exercise of lynch law as Stephen
suffered. The Jewish authorities were not entitled to impose
sentences of death (Jn. xviii.31); these were reserved to the
Romans. The Supreme Council, taking care to avoid any
further overstepping of its authority, proceeded against the
Christians by imposing sentences of imprisonment and corporal
punishment. The confusion into which the Church was thrown
was so great as to force a section of it to flee the city. The
apostles remained, and with them, we may presume, the group
of conservative-minded Jewish Christians from Palestine. The
Christians among the Jews of the Diaspora went back to the
"Dispersion," that is, the Diaspora (Acts viii.1, 4); to these
belonged Philip, who baptised the Ethiopian eunuch (Acts
viii.26ff.); they comprised especially the unknown men of
Cyprus and Cyrene who dared to take the first step towards
founding a Christian mission to the Gentiles, and set up the
first Gentile Christian Church in Syrian Antioch (Acts xi.19ff.)
Many appear to have made for Damascus; at any rate, that is
where Saul wished to go in order to help exterminate the hated
brood of Nazarenes even beyond the borders of Judaea. Letters
of recommendation from the Supreme Council were intended
to facilitate his entry into the synagogues in Damascus. So Paul
set off with a few companions to cover the distance of approximately a hundred and thirty-five miles by foot or on an ass—
probably not on horseback. Damascus at that time was Roman;
even today the so-called "Triumphal Arch" near the wonderful
Omayyad Mosque remains, along with others, an impressive
memorial of that period. Saul was already near his goal; the

roofs of the city shone before him in the brilliant midday sun.
Then it was that something wonderful, inconceivable occurred;
an unearthly light threw Paul to the ground; he heard a voice;
dazed, he got to his feet again, and, blinded, the former persecutor allowed himself to be led by his companions as a
prisoner of Christ into the city.

What actually happened? Paul himself gives only a very few
hints. He is not in the habit of saying much about his own
experiences; with him every stress is laid upon the proclamation
of Christ. Only occasionally does a recollection of the Damascus experience shine through. As the basis of his apostolate
Paul maintains to the Corinthians: "Have I not seen Jesus our
Lord?" (1 Cor. ix.1). This can only refer to the hour before
Damascus, for an encounter with Jesus before his conversion
would in this connexion have been inconclusive. On another
occasion Paul equates his Damascus experience with the Easter
experiences of the first disciples (1 Cor. xv.8). It concerns an
appearance of the risen Christ without any closer indication
being given of the nature of this appearance. It is merely
placed in clear relationship to his previous activity as a persecutor of the Christians (1 Cor. xv.9), which again speaks for a
recollection of Damascus. In another place he sums up the
ineffable content of that hour in one profoundly simple phrase:
"Christ Jesus has made me his own" (Phil. iii.12). The statement: "God was pleased . . . to reveal his Son in me" (Gal.
1.15f., mg.) has almost a modern psychological ring. There is
no question here of any external influence; the whole thing may
be interpreted as an event which took place entirely within
Paul. That he was here thinking of Damascus is suggested by
the statement in the following verse: "And again I returned to
Damascus" (Gal. 1.17). One wonderful passage, ii Cor. iv.6,
speaks of an inner light: "It is the God who said, 'Let light
shine out of darkness' who has shone in our hearts to give the
light of the knowledge of the glory of God in the face of Christ."
Whether Paul was speaking particularly of his own experience
before Damascus, or whether he was thinking rather of a
general Christian experience cannot clearly be seen; probably
the latter is the case. Nevertheless the image may have
been suggested to him by the memory of Damascus. At
any rate, it was as a new creation, comparable with that

D

first day of Creation, that Paul experienced his conversion.

Acts gives an account of Paul's conversion in three passages:
(1) in the course of its historical narrative (Acts IX.1-9);
(2) in Paul's speech before the Jews in Jerusalem (Acts XXII.3-11);
(3) in Paul's speech before Agrippa and Festus at Caesarea by
the sea (Acts XXVI.12-18). The three accounts agree in essential
details. The most notable peculiarity of the third account is the
reference to kicking against the goads. The effect upon Paul's
companions is related variously: according to IX.7 they hear
the voice but see nothing; according to XXII.9 they see the light
but do not hear the voice; and according to XXVI.14 they fall to
the ground. Yet these are petty details which carry no great
weight. That Luke introduces the variations at all will be due
to the fact that he himself had various accounts at his disposal
as sources for his "Acts of the Apostles," and that he did not
wish to neglect any one form of the tradition in favour of
another. More important is the fundamental question whether
we must not take account of the possibility of legendary
accretions in all three accounts. This is naturally very likely
with such an occurrence as this, which it would certainly be
difficult to put into words. What Paul heard before Damascus
may well have been "things that cannot be told, which man
may not utter" (II Cor. XII.4). Nevertheless, what Acts men-
tions as being the words of the "voice" would correspond more
or less to what was actually said. This already follows from the
significance attached to the event. The question of how we are
to picture the light from heaven is not so vital. The accounts
themselves diverge quite notably upon this point. The main
thing is that for Paul this "Light" was an enlightenment. We
need have no anxieties on this score if we are able to interpret
the narrative in Acts as merely a description of the outward and
visible aspects of an internal event. Spiritual happenings are
no less real than material ones. Christ was working in him just
as substantially as in an event of the physical world. But, in a
manner similar to art, the Bible likes to portray spiritual
happenings in a physical, concrete form. How otherwise is one
to portray them without employing colourless abstractions and
falling prey to the "pale cast of thought." Here we touch upon
recognition of the parabolic character of word and gesture,
indeed of physical representation as a whole. In no way does

the mention of Paul's blindness militate against the interpretation of the story as a spiritual event. We know that grave
mental shocks very often have physical consequences. For the
rest we must be very cautious in our historical judgment where
such happenings are concerned, for they defy every attempt at
crude analysis. Historically the event as such is well established;
how otherwise could the sudden change in Paul be explained?
That alone is what really matters; we need not concern ourselves with the form of the event in detail. Only one modern
misconception must be cleared away: a spiritual happening of
this kind cannot be attributed simply to imagination. Naturally
there are psychical phenomena which can only be symptoms of
a diseased imagination, and these are termed hallucinations.
But has one ever heard of a diseased imagination bringing
about a man's spiritual recovery? In any case, the Apostle does
not give the impression of being a morbid fanatic, but rather a
man of action who, with his message of Christ, has his feet
firmly upon the ground. The assessment of such a spiritual
experience will always depend upon its effects. If we see the
workings of God in Paul's life-achievement, then we shall also
perceive that the spiritual starting-point of this work was
divinely perpetrated. If, however, we consider Paul's activity
to be one great error, and dismiss his preaching as fanciful, then
it will be impossible now or ever to prove that his spiritual
experience near Damascus was God's work. Again, if we interpreted the Apostle's preaching of Christ as nothing but
cleverly-disguised Jewish propaganda, we would never be
persuaded of the historical reality of the spiritual experience of
that hour. We would also dismiss Paul's references to his conversion as clever fiction. Of course, over and against such distortion of the historical picture of Paul there stands the simple
fact that in Paul's letters we can trace Jesus's spirit of truthful-
ness throughout. A man who is subject to the dominion of
Jesus does not base his work upon a colossal lie. Thus we shall
have to judge the nature of the Damascus experience in the
light of Paul's work, the tremendous historical impact of which
is clearly manifest, and cannot be disputed by any thinking
man. One's verdict will, of course, differ according to one's
personal attitude. The man who will not acknowledge the
evidence of the Spirit and of the power animating this work,

cannot be compelled to do so. However, the man who senses that through contact with the world of Paul he is drawing nearer to God, will likewise believe the utterances of this man whose conversion experience he interprets as the Father drawing him, Paul, to the Son. This view, which is firmly based upon fundamentals, is wholly compatible with an open-minded attitude towards the individual details of the historical account in Acts.

What, however, is the actual content of this conversion? This must now be formulated more precisely. We have seen above that Paul, the scribe and Pharisee, took twofold exception to the message of Christ: (1) A crucified man could not be the Messiah, the emissary of God; (2) With His preaching of God's love for the sinner Jesus abrogated the Law. Correspondingly we have the twofold light that was bestowed upon Paul through the Damascus experience: (1) Christ was alive, and the Crucified also the Risen. Indeed He had appeared to him both as alive and as Lord. The reality of the Living One was greater than what he had hitherto thought of as life. It was a reality from which he could no longer flee; it had taken possession of him. God had acknowledged Him whom Israel had rejected. (2) His zeal for the Law and his boasting about righteousness had made him a sinner; his religious fanaticism had led him into murder. His path was marked by hatred and bloodthirstiness, but Christ waylaid him not, however, to annihilate him, but to draw him to Himself and to enlist him in His service. The miracle of grace that the proud Pharisee would not credit became a reality in his life; Christ accepted him, the sinner. "Where sin increased, grace abounded all the more" (Rom. v.20). The Law may hitherto have been the only possible road by which man could reach God, but it had not led to the goal. Then it was that God in His unfathomable mercy set out on the road to men. Christ was this road of God's to men. At the point where man's road came to an end there, precisely there, stood Christ, and now began the march in the opposite direction. Grace called Paul into service, and thereby showed itself to be true grace.

This double perception which was thereby bestowed upon Paul also forms the twofold theme of his apostolic preaching. This theme is summed up in the words "Easter" and "Justification." Both had become Paul's most personal certainties and express nothing but his most individual experience. "Easter"—that meant "Christ lives!" The divine miracle has become reality, the invasion of the divine world into this dispensation has taken place. The old world is in the process of dying; life retains the victory. The powers of the coming era are at work. The forces of darkness have been disarmed, however unruly they may appear. In the light of Easter the song of triumph may ring out: "O death, where is thy victory? O death, where is thy sting?" (1 Cor. xv.55). For what Christ has here fought for and won He does not wish to keep to Himself. He wants to share the spoils; we have only to allow that they be given to us. Whoever falls in after Christ has the right to take part in His triumphal procession. Whoever is "in Christ" has all things in common with Him. "Therefore, if any one is in Christ, he is a new creation; the old has passed away, behold, the new has come" (II Cor. v.17).

This leads on to the second theme of Paul's preaching: "Justification." The doctrine of Justification answers the question: How can I become right with God? The Jew replies: By the works of the Law. To him this is the righteousness that avails with God (cf. Rom. 1.17). Paul perceived that we can never become righteous, that is, right with God, in this way, for "Cursed be he who does not confirm the words of this law by doing them" (Deut. xxvii.26, Gal. iii.10). But who can say of himself that he does not stand under this curse? Who keeps the Law in every respect? "As it is written: 'None is righteous, no, not one;'" (Rom. iii.10, cf. Ps. xiv.3). Thus the Law is doubtless holy (Rom. vii.12), but it does not make us holy. It has no power to cut us off from our sin and take us out of our old existence. Indeed, it belongs itself to the old era, the old dispensation. At this point, however, the Easter message comes into operation. With Christ the new world, God's world, has dawned. In this new world the Law, which itself belongs to the old world, can no longer make a man righteous, indeed it has no longer any need to do so. The Law was "our custodian until Christ came . . . But now that faith has come, we are no longer under a custodian" (Gal. iii.24f.) For now "apart from the law" the righteousness has been manifested which avails with God (Rom. iii.21). The man who belongs to Christ belongs to the new world; he is right with God. Christ is thus the end of the Law; "every one who has faith" in Him (*i.e.* everyone who belongs to Him, who is united with Him, who is "in Christ") is righteous (Rom. x.4). The man who desired to attempt this by way of the Law would not acknowledge Christ, God's road to men. But the man who desired to set his own deed higher than God's deed and not acknowledge Christ would not be right with God (Rom. x.3). For "Christ Jesus . . . God made . . . our righteousness" (1 Cor. 1.30), "so that in him we might become the righteousness of God" (II Cor. v.21). That is "Justification by faith"—not an achievement of man, but acceptance of the divine gift. Paul is thus able to describe the new "righteousness" as "sonship" (Rom. VIII.14f., Gal. IV.5). The true child does not boast, like the Pharisee, of his achievements (Rom. III.27), but is a child precisely because he lets his father provide him with everything. The Pauline doctrine of Justification is none other than an interpretation of the Parable of the Prodigal Son in the light of Easter. In the resurrection of Christ God Himself has uttered this divine "Amen" to Jesus's preaching of God's love for sinners. Damascus, because it is Paul's Easter experience, entails for him the experience of justification at the same time. Both these things point back to Christ Himself. Damascus, therefore, is simply Paul's experience of Christ. His old being has passed away; his new life is a "being-in-Christ" (Gal. II.20). This has also been called Paul's "Christ-mysticism." We may dispute the expression, but we easily understand what is meant by it. This Christ-mysticism feeds on the Easter fact; it is a sharing in the death and resurrection of Christ (Rom. VI.4), and thus embraces justification. In Christ-mysticism the twofold theme of Paul's preaching finds its unity.

# THE PREPARATION

PAUL had set off for Damascus as a persecutor; he entered Damascus as a prisoner of Christ. He reached his destination, though other than he had dreamed. He groped as a blind man for the hands of his companions. Hitherto the leader, he had to learn to let himself be guided. This detail of the narrative strikes us as a parable of his future career. "Take Thou my hand and guide me" became the watchword of his wanderings. His own path had ended before Damascus; from now on he moved in "imitation of Christ." Paul became an apostle, that is, an ambassador, one who does not journey on his own account but on that of his master; who does not deliver his own message but that of his king; who does not act on his own authority but with the warrant of a superior. The school into which he had been received was no easy one for Paul. In it he had first to learn to resign himself and wait humbly for orders. The impulsiveness which he demonstrated even in the hour of his conversion was for once checked. The new convert's stormy question, "What shall I do, Lord?" was followed by the sobering reply, "Rise, and go into Damascus; and there you will be told all that is appointed for you to do" (Acts xxii.10). Did Paul, it is to be wondered, already then understand the educational wisdom of this reply? First love is quickly fired to great deeds; but the test of its sincerity lies in simple obedience and the readiness to forego spectacular achievements. Paul would later do great deeds in the service of his Master. But these deeds were no longer to find their deepest justification in the natural impulse of a man of action who had never been thwarted; this impulsiveness had to be taken "captive to obey Christ" (ii Cor. x.5). The urge to achievement had to pass first through the hard school of deprivation; in this way the Apostle overcame the temptation to "boast." "For if I preach the gospel, that gives me no ground for boasting. For necessity is laid upon me. Woe to me if I do not preach the gospel!" (i Cor. ix.16). This obedience found its final proof in the readiness to lay down life itself, for the Lord had agreed with this "chosen instrument" on these terms: "I will show him how much he must suffer for the sake of my name" (Acts ix.15f.) Possibly this road, which led "through many tribulations" into "the kingdom of God" (Acts xiv.22) was not as yet clear to the newly-won disciple as he took his first steps along it. Later he recognised and affirmed joyfully the "law under which he had entered." For this law was none other than the Law of Christ Himself: "He humbled himself and became obedient unto death, even death on a cross" (Phil. ii.8). How on earth could the Apostle have preached the message of the Cross had he not borne the Cross in his Master's wake! And so finally he boasts of his weaknesses, "that the power of Christ may rest upon" him (ii Cor. xii.9). The man who perceives in this the "ethics of the weakling" is like a blind man talking about colour. He has no idea of the depths of divine wisdom over which he ignorantly strides. From a human point of view, Paul undoubtedly belongs to the ranks of the "strong." The Apostle put his finger on his most vital quality when he boasted of his weakness. Without Christ he would not have found it. Only in the light of Christ's Cross and Resurrection did the divine secret disclose itself to him: "Power is made perfect in weakness" (ii Cor. xii.9).

According to the account in the Acts of the Apostles (ix.10ff.), Paul lodged in Damascus with a certain Judas. His house was situated in the "Straight Street," which is probably to be identified with the mile-long highway which runs through Damascus from east to west. Three days he lingered there without taking food (Acts ix.9), quite overwhelmed by the sight which had befallen him. The man called by God to great things is caused, at first, to be quite alone. But, out of the loneliness following this most deeply shattering experience, Paul's way led into fellowship. A simple and otherwise unknown Christian called Ananias was chosen to bring this great one in the Kingdom of God into the Church. From his mouth Paul heard the greeting, later so familiar to him, of "brother." Under his encouragement the dreadful tension of the past few days relaxed; his lost eyesight returned and through Paul's baptism the seal was set upon the hour. The statement in Galatians 1.15-17 in no way contradicts this account of events. If Paul there ascribes the origin of his Christian life entirely to

God's initiative and appears to exclude every human agency, that is intended to serve as a clarification of his relationship to the first apostles. Not through them had Paul turned to Christianity, nor was the form of his Christianity determined by them. He stands alongside them independently as one who received his Christianity directly from the Lord (Gal. 1.11f.) But that does not necessarily rule out Ananias's simple act of service, for his opponents (Gal.1.7, VI.12) certainly did not try to score off him by charging him with dependence upon Ananias.

In addition to Acts we must draw upon Paul's own account in the first chapter of his letter to the Galatians for subsequent events. His first stay in Damascus presumably lasted only a short time, and it is questionable whether he became acquainted on that occasion with the local church, as Acts IX.19 states. Actually this probably refers to his second stay in Damascus, though the picture in Acts is not clear on this point. Paul himself writes; "I went away into Arabia" (Gal.1.17). "Arabia" was the name given at that time to the whole Arabian Peninsula as far as the Gates of Damascus, just as Jordan today bears the proud title, "Kingdom of Arabia." The reference in Galatians 1.17 is probably to the former kingdom of Nabatea, "Stony Arabia," whose chief cities of Petra, Gerasa and Amman (Philadelphia) still surprise and astonish the visitor with their magnificent relics of the Graeco-Roman period. The solitude of the territory, which was sparsely populated, would have attracted Paul, in order that here, in the quiet of the edge of the desert, he might ponder the weightiest decision of his life. Tent-making was practised then as now in that region; it is quite conceivable that Paul earned his living at this time by means of this, the trade in which he had become skilled. This voluntary self-exile cannot be dissociated from Paul's development. It was the necessary period of preparation before the beginning of his great task. All great tasks for the Kingdom of God ripen secretly. Augustine withdrew after his conversion into the quiet of a country estate in order to give himself entirely to contemplation. Luther's reforming insight matured in the seclusion of his monastic cell. Even our Lord Himself, prior to His public ministry, was led into the desert by the Spirit (Mt. IV.1). We are probably not to think of Paul undertaking any missionary activity during this time of preparation. His company was with the Bible, which he now read with new eyes. For him the "veil" over the Old Testament was lifted after the "glory of the Lord" had mirrored itself in his heart. The ministry of the letter, which he had served as a scribe, was transformed for him into the ministry of the Spirit which gives life (II Cor. III.6-18). The bondage to precepts under which he had lived as a Pharisee had to give way to the "glorious liberty of the children of God" (Rom. VIII.21).

We do not know how long Paul stayed in "Arabia." There is no evidence for the popular belief that it was three years. We shall have to think in terms rather of months than of years. "And again I returned to Damascus" (Gal. 1.17). The passage Acts IX.19-25 relates to this second sojourn in Damascus. It was now that Paul began his missionary preaching. He directed his attention first of all to the Jews, as he did later still on his missionary travels. In the synagogue anyone could come forward and speak if he felt he had anything to say. Paul did not wish to let this opportunity slip. He sought to prove to his co-religionists that Jesus was the Messiah. We notice that he had meanwhile studied the scriptures on the subject. Paul had recourse to the Jews because he himself belonged to them. In his opinion the story of Jesus applied first and foremost to them. In Christ the expectations of the Old Covenant were fulfilled. Yet, already, here in Damascus, Paul had to endure the disappointment which recurred time and again thereafter and was one of the bitterest experiences of his life (cf. Rom. IX-XI); it was particularly the Jews who rejected the message of Christ. Amazement over the inner transformation of the former persecutor of the Christians soon turned into wild hatred towards the apostate. Plans were laid: Paul had to be destroyed. To that end the Jews had won round none other than the Ethnarch (governor) of the Nabatean king Aretas of Petra, probably by means of bribery (cf. II Cor. XI.32f.) The underlying historical circumstances are not entirely clear. Was Damascus then, as formerly, Roman, or had it come temporarily into the possession of Aretas? Suffice it to say that they were lying in wait for Paul. The Christians heard of the plan and, in buccaneer fashion, Paul was let down the city wall in a basket by night and escaped into the open. For the first time he was forced to face the fact that his road as an ambassador for Christ was continually to take him perilously close to death. That was in the third year after his conversion (Gal. 1.18)—the ancient method of counting included the year of commencement as a full year.

Paul turned towards Jerusalem. What could have induced him to take this step? He gives as his reason: I wanted to visit Peter in order to get to know him (Gal. 1.18). Besides Peter, Paul further made the acquaintance of the new leader of the Church, James, the Lord's brother. We do not know when James joined the Church. In any event it appears that he had had a special Easter experience (1. Cor. xv.7). The fact that we meet him here alongside Peter and later alone as leader of the Church links up with the re-grouping of the Jerusalem Church after the death of Stephen. James was known for his fidelity to the Law and carried weight even in Pharisaic circles. We may presume that after the scattering of the Hellenists (Acts viii.1) the conservative element in the mother church again wished to lay greater stress upon what they had in common with Judaism. The choice of James as leader of the Church is to be viewed from this standpoint. In addition, his kinship with the Lord would also have played an important part. Paul explicitly denies having seen any of the other apostles (Gal. 1.19), and insists that he had remained personally unknown to the churches in Judaea to which pre-eminently Jerusalem belonged (Gal. 1.22). An obvious contradiction exists at this point between the testimony of Paul and the account in Acts (ix.26-29). According to Acts Paul went in and out with the first apostles in Jerusalem, and aroused the opposition of the Diaspora Jews there with his public preaching; indeed, only by timely flight was he able to escape the fate of Stephen. These two accounts cannot, by any stretch of the imagination, be reconciled, and it is clear that in this case the testimony of Paul is to be preferred to Luke's account. Paul, it is true, writes in great excitement and with a definite aim, namely, to demonstrate the independence of his apostolate from the first apostles; but his solemn assurance that he was speaking the truth must be taken seriously, and in any case the Apostle had a more reliable view of events than the later tradition.

Many a reader may experience difficulty in acknowledging

such contradictions in the New Testament. Yet it is certainly
not God's will that we should shut our eyes to a clearly recognised truth, nor shall we be any the more pious for doing so.
We must consider where the real importance of the Bible lies.
It is not a history book, whose worth depends on its historical
reliability. The Bible is intended to lead us to God by showing
us God's road to men. This task the Bible has fulfilled, and will
in all ages fulfil. It is of no vital importance if this or that
historical error creeps into its portrayal of events, nor does it in
the slightest way alter its real significance. We can therefore
quietly accept even the contradiction just indicated, without
being obliged, on that account, to be sceptical about the whole
Bible.

The note to the effect that Barnabas took it upon himself to
introduce Paul to the apostles in Jerusalem (Acts ix.27) can, in
fact, be reconciled with the account in Galatians, where Paul
had no reason to mention it explicitly. Later we meet this
Barnabas frequently in the company of Paul. His name was
actually Joseph; the surname "Barnabas" is Aramaic and probably means "Son of encouragement" (Acts iv.36f.) He was a
Levite from Cyprus, thus belonging to the Judaism of the Diaspora, but he early found his way into the primitive Church,
where he became well remembered for his magnanimous acts
of love. According to what we shall hear about him later on,
he became one of the most significant personalities in the early
Church. Even such a man as Paul had to submit to his leadership in the first place, and even after their separation (Acts xv.
36ff.) spoke of him with respect (1 Cor. ix.6).

Yet another noteworthy experience of Paul's falls into the
period of his fourteen-day stay in Jerusalem, though mentioned
in quite another context, namely his speech of defence before
the Jews in Jerusalem (Acts xxii.17-21). According to this, it
was obviously Paul's intention to appear in the Hellenistic
synagogues in Jerusalem preaching Christ. It was there, where
his opposition to Stephen would still be remembered freshly,
that his preaching could not fail to have an impact—or so he
thought. But in a vision of Christ which he received during a
trance in prayer, it became clear to him that his destiny was
rather to bring the joyful news to the Gentiles instead. So Paul
left Jerusalem, and he may thereby have met the wishes of the

mother church, for whom his presence would have become the occasion of new disturbances and persecutions.

Paul then turned towards his home-town of Tarsus in Cilicia (Acts ix.30, Gal. 1.21). We know nothing at all of this period. We do not know how long it lasted or what Paul did during it. Did he quietly begin his missionary work? Do the churches of Cilicia mentioned in Acts xv.41 owe their existence to him? Or did he once again have to restrain himself? Was he once more obliged to curb the impatience of his missionary zeal in order to mature still further in solitude for his great task? Did his Master have to impose a waiting period upon him in order to exercise him in the patience which was to be so necessary for him in his later work (ii. Cor. vi.4)? We can give no certain answer to any of these questions; there is therefore no value in pursuing idle speculations in this matter.

Not until Acts xi.25 do we again reach the solid ground of historical certainty. We are there told that the above-mentioned Barnabas sought out Paul in Tarsus in order to secure his collaboration in the work of the Church at Syrian Antioch. Paul agreed to go with him and the joint activity of the two men in Antioch lasted a whole year (Acts xi.26, Gal. 1.21). In this metropolis unknown Jewish Christians had founded the first Gentile-Christian "metropolis." The step towards a mission to the Gentiles had been taken, and with it an unexpected development had begun. The Church flourished. In Jerusalem they took notice of this new centre of the Christian faith. In order to establish contact with it they sent the most suitable man that they had, namely Barnabas; with him went Paul. The activity in Antioch was the best conceivable preparation for the future effectiveness of the Apostle among the Gentiles. Antioch was a metropolis of over half a million inhabitants, the third largest city in the Roman Empire. The pride of the city were its two intersecting colonnaded streets, as well as its ingenious water and garden devices. The Antiochenes' lust for pleasure and enjoyment was both famous and infamous. The jostling of different nationalities in one city may have furthered this tendency to debauchery and preoccupation with immorality. Romans, Greeks, Syrians and Jews formed the chief elements in the population at that time. So whereas Tarsus, the home of Paul, was a centre of ancient culture,

Antioch was primarily a commercial city. Paul here had the opportunity to become acquainted with the social and moral needs of a metropolis; he could here prove whether the joyful news of Christ contained the power to be the salvation of a whole world. The beginnings of the church in Antioch appear to have been promising. Indeed, the metropolis began to take notice of the disciples and called them contemptuously "Christians" (Acts XI.26). In Palestine the followers of Jesus were called Nazarenes; the first evidence of the name "Christian" is to be found in Antioch.

In connexion with the activity of Paul and Barnabas, Acts records a journey that the two men made to Jerusalem with alms (Acts XI.27-30, XII.25). Economic difficulties had arisen in the church at Jerusalem, a result, probably, of the pooling of goods that had been carried through there. The enthusiastic ardour of their love, counting upon the imminent coming of the Lord, had all too daringly overleaped the ordinances of this world. This had in time led to abuses; now, moreover, a famine was threatening. The church in Antioch, which clearly lived in better economic circumstances than the church in Jerusalem, took it as a matter of course that they should express their gratitude to the mother church by the granting of practical help. Barnabas and Paul carried the proceeds of the collection to Jerusalem. But the account of this alms journey does not agree with the Apostle's own account of the journey, in Galatians. The second journey to Jerusalem that is there mentioned (Gal. II.1ff.) naturally relates to the events of Acts xv, the so-called Apostolic Council in Jerusalem. We can hardly presume that Paul would have simply omitted from his account the "alms journey" of Acts XI.27-30, neither would it have been freely invented by the writer of Acts. Accordingly, one tries to meet this difficulty with the explanation that it is to be identified with the journey mentioned in Acts xv.1ff., which of course only creates new difficulties, for the motive of this journey reads quite differently. We must content ourselves with the fact that many events in the history of the early Church are no longer, or not as yet, clearly discernible.

# THE FIRST MISSIONARY JOURNEY

THE title "The Acts of the Apostles" is misleading. This book in no way presents a history of the apostles. Of the apostles only Peter and Paul stand in the forefront of the narrative; John is mentioned in passing as the companion of Peter (Acts III.1ff., VIII.14); the martyrdom of his brother, James, is reported (Acts XII.2); and some references are made to James, the brother of our Lord, but that is all. Apparently the fate of the "Twelve" is of no interest to Acts, or else it has no information on the subject. Acts cannot even be termed a double biography of Peter and Paul. Peter disappears from the field of vision with Acts XII.17, and reappears only momentarily, in Acts XV. The puzzling and much discussed conclusion of Acts (XXVIII.30f.) leaves us with innumerable unanswered questions regarding the further fate of Paul. A serious biography could never end thus. But that is just what Acts does not set out to be. The Acts of the Apostles is not concerned with the apostles as such; it does not in any way wish to glorify them or place them in the centre of the picture. Acts is much more the story of the ascended Christ. All the stories in it are stories of Christ, even where they tell of the deeds of the apostles. For these deeds do not purport to be anything other than the work of Christ; and this work, to which the apostles are committed, consists, first and foremost, of the spreading of the Gospel. How is the Gospel to reach the Gentiles? That is the question which concerns the Acts of the Apostles. The story of the ascended Christ in His Church is the theme of Acts; the triumphal progress of the Gospel from Jerusalem to Rome, from the centre of the Old Covenant to the centre of the world, is its content.

The narratives in Acts of Paul's missionary journeys are likewise to be read from this standpoint. He does not undertake these journeys on his own initiative, but on the instructions of Christ. It is Christ who is at work in this journey of the Apostle through the ancient world; the Apostle is only the "ambassador" of Christ. Christ's work occurs where the Apostle

"worked harder than any of them" (1 Cor. xv.10), and this fact
is laid down with great emphasis at the commencement of his
missionary activity. That is the significance, we may assume,
of the strange account of the sending out of Paul and Barnabas
on the mission (Acts xiii.1-3). Amid fasting and prayer the
leaders of the church in Antioch, who are mentioned by name,
heard the voice of the divine Spirit directing them to Paul and
Barnabas. Having heard this voice they felt no doubt and no
hesitation. They were themselves Spirit-bearers ("prophets"),
and as such they imparted to the two men chosen to be missionaries the gift of the divine Spirit by the laying-on of hands. To
many modern readers this story may seem somewhat strange.
Our present-day generation tends to adopt a sceptical attitude
to the genuineness of such immediate divine intuitions. But
the fact that we do not have such experiences does not give us
some sort of absolute right to deny that others have them. In
the early Church the Holy Spirit was no pale abstraction but a
most vital experienced reality, and we shall come across several
more examples of the same thing. Instead of prematurely
criticising such experiences we should rather ask ourselves why
we have to such a great extent lost them. This does not mean,
of course, commending "enthusiasm," for such experiences
cannot be compelled to take place, and such is the altered outlook of modern man that he cannot forego critical examination
of the facts.

Barnabas and Paul were joined by John, surnamed Mark,
who became their companion (Acts xii.25, xiii.13). He was a
cousin of Barnabas (Col. iv.10), and the son of a Christian
woman, Mary, in whose house the early Church apparently
came together regularly (Acts xii.12). According to an old
tradition he wrote the second Gospel at the behest of Peter, and
is supposed to be the fleeing youth who is mentioned only in
Mark's Gospel (Mk. xiv.51f.) His separation from Paul (Acts
xiii.13, xv.36ff.) did not seem to cause any final estrangement,
for Mark appears again later in Paul's circle (Col. iv.10,
Philem. 24; cf. ii Tim, iv.11), and in Peter's also (1 Pet. v.13).
In the early Church he was accounted the first bishop of
Alexandria.

The first destination of the three missionaries was the island
of Cyprus, the home of Barnabas (Acts iv.36). The latter cir-

cumstance may have been decisive for Barnabas, who appears, to begin with, as the leader of the expedition. It is not certain whether Paul had originally set himself a further goal, though it may be assumed (cf. Acts XIII.13, XV.39-41). In any event he complied at first with the wishes of Barnabas. They embarked at Seleucia, the harbour of Antioch, and, to this day, the two moles bear the names of Paul and Barnabas. After a good two days they reached Cyprus and landed at Salamis, the former capital of the island, a few miles north of the present-day Famagusta. Cyprus is a fertile island, rich in timber, minerals and metals; it gave its name to the copper first discovered there. The Phoenicians had already set foot on the island, but it later became totally Hellenised. Innumerable Jews lived there, lured by the trade in metal. Barnabas and Paul were thus able to seek out several synagogues in Salamis in order to preach the news of Christ. In view of Acts XI.19 it is probable that Christian churches had already been founded in Cyprus; to them a strengthening by Paul and Barnabas would have been highly welcome. We may estimate the stay in Salamis to have lasted a few weeks, though Acts is silent on this point. The next halt that Acts names was likewise the terminus of the apostles' activities on Cyprus: Paphos, situated on the western edge of the island (Acts XIII.6-12), a good ninety miles, as the crow flies, from Salamis. The old city was known for its shrine to Aphrodite, who here bore a resemblance to the Phoenician goddess Astarte, the celebration of whose cult took the lowest and most sensual forms. The old city was a ruin even in Paul's day; its place had been taken by New Paphos, at that time the residence of the Roman proconsul, Lucius Sergius Paulus, who appears, from extra-biblical information, to have been a man of varied interests. It is very likely that he had already heard something of the Christian message, and this offers the best explanation of the appearance before him of Paul and Barnabas, which led to a dramatic scene. In the proconsul's circle lived a Jewish magician, whose name has been transmitted variously as Elymas, Barjesus, and Hetoimas. Occultism was no less widespread at the time of the Roman Empire than it is today; then as now many a swindler made profitable business out of the occult tendencies of his contemporaries. This Elymas anticipated unwelcome competition from the apostles. In return he

E

was delivered up to divine punishment by Paul, who from here onwards is referred to only by his Roman name (Acts. XIII.9). The narrative, which has its exact parallel in the dispute between Peter and Simon Magus (Acts VIII 9ff.), has a strongly Old Testament flavour. Paul in his zeal resembles Elijah or one of the prophets. In this story the bitter struggle which the early Christians waged against the "magic world-view" is actualised. There could be no confusing of Christianity with these dark intrigues; only a hard, clean break would suffice. In the audience with the proconsul Paul appears for the first time as the leader alongside Barnabas, a fact which stands out increasingly clearly from then on. He presumably determined the further goal of their journeys, the interior of Asia Minor, which was to be opened up to the Christian Gospel. This possibly went beyond what had originally been agreed; such at any rate would be the easiest explanation of John Mark's departure.

Once again the account in Acts is very sketchy. It merely names three points: Paphos in Cyprus, Perga in Pamphylia (in the south of Asia Minor) and Antioch in Pisidia (not to be confused with Antioch in Syria). We must not imagine this "journey" to have been particularly pleasant. To reach Antioch from Perga, Paul and Barnabas had to cross the Taurus. A harsh mountain climate prevailed here, while dangerous fever-mists lay upon the Pamphylian plain. Attention has rightly been drawn recently to the variations in height of the places touched by Paul. Tarsus and Antioch lie only 260 feet above sea-level, Damascus, on the other hand, 2,250 feet; Jerusalem 2,570 feet; Pisidian Antioch 3,900 feet; Iconium 3,340 feet; Lystra 4,000 feet. We must take these variations in height into account when measuring the sheer physical achievement that lay behind Paul's journeys. In addition there were sometimes very unfavourable travelling conditions generally. This applies especially to the crossing of the Taurus. Through wild and lonely ravines the rough path led steeply upwards. The region was notorious for the robber bands which lurked there. Paul must have come across them either then or later. A river constituted yet another obstacle upon his road. Bridges were non-existent; there was no alternative but to swim across, or at least to wade across—not always a safe procedure!

"Just measure out the mileage which Paul travelled by water and land, and yourself try to follow the course of his journeys. You sit, with your visa on your passport, and your diplomatic recommendations in your pocket, in a comfortable modern carriage on the Anatolian railway, and travel in the evening twilight easily towards your destination on the permanent way which has been forced through rocks and over streams by engineering skill and dynamite. While, having already booked your rooms by telegraph, you are carried rapidly and without effort over the pass, you see, in the fading light of evening, the ancient road, narrow and stony, that climbs the pass, and upon that road a few people on foot and riding donkeys, or in exceptional cases perhaps on horseback, are hurrying along towards the crowded, dirty inn. They are bound to reach it before darkness finally settles in, for the night is no friend to man; the wild dogs of the inhospitable shepherds set themselves raging in the way, robbers are ready to take money, clothes, and beasts, and the demons of fever threaten the overheated and weary in the cold night wind, which is already blowing down from the side valleys."[1]

Paul was probably not exaggerating when, looking back upon the manifold hardships of his life, he wrote: "On frequent journeys, in danger from rivers, danger from robbers, danger from my own people, danger from Gentiles, danger in the city, danger in the wilderness, danger at sea, danger from false brethren; in toil and hardship, through many a sleepless night, in hunger and thirst, often without food, in cold and exposure" (II Cor. XI.26f.)

The strenuous march of the two emissaries of Christ would have taken about six days. They then saw Pisidian Antioch lying before them. The remains of a vast Roman aqueduct recall its golden age even today. The emperor Augustus had planted a colony of veterans in the city, which originated in the Seleucid period. The interior of Asia Minor was thus opened up in a peaceful manner to Graeco-Roman culture. There was also a Jewish community in this city, which was rich in trade and commerce.

The account of Paul's activity in Antioch gives a typical picture of his missionary method (Acts XIII.14-52). Paul and

[1] A. Deissmann, *Paul*, tr. W. E. Wilson, London 1926, pp. 63f.

Barnabas presumably took lodgings in the Jewish quarter. As it was the Sabbath, they both betook themselves to the synagogue. In company with the Jews we also see many half-proselytes, called in Acts "God-fearers." These were Gentiles who had adopted Jewish worship, without, however, assuming the whole Law and, in particular, circumcision. The synagogues of the Diaspora were at that time the rallying points for such religiously inclined Gentiles. After the scripture-reading Paul and Barnabas were invited to come forward and speak. They had been recognised immediately as strangers, possibly even as rabbis. At this point Luke offers a model example of an address such as Paul may have frequently delivered on other similar occasions in the synagogue. Certain passages echo Peter's Pentecost sermon (cf. Acts XIII.38), others recall ideas from Romans. The address links up with the Messianic hope and demonstrates its fulfilment in Jesus Christ. Christ, however, bestows the righteousness which the Law of Moses could never procure.

The address made a strong impression, so much so that on the next Sabbath the synagogue was full to overflowing. The Gentiles sensed that Paul had something in particular to say to them. It was precisely this which provoked the Jews to opposition. In their minds they saw the proselytes and Gentiles straying after this new preaching. They saw through the situation: this Paul was to become their most dangerous competitor. He would reap where they had sown (Jn. IV.37f.) Was their work to have been in vain? No, never! But amidst the resulting commotion a decision of world-wide importance was made: "It was necessary that the word of God should be spoken first to you. Since you thrust it from you, and judge yourselves unworthy of eternal life, behold, we turn to the Gentiles" (Acts XIII.46).

These words give expression to the programme of the Pauline message. It was directed in the first place to the Jews. Paul always sought out the synagogues first, for they offered, of course, the natural points of contact for his preaching. Here he met not only his erstwhile fellow-believers, but also the Gentiles, who would be sure to give him a ready hearing. Moreover his preaching thereby came under the legal protection which was granted to the synagogue in respect of its proselytising activity. But the decision which was made in Antioch and the separation which took place as a result were also typical of Paul's missionary work. We meet the Jews everywhere as fanatical opponents of the Apostle. But, although pursued by their boundless hatred, he took the Gospel to the Gentiles. So Christianity became a world religion.

Paul's preaching was not in vain. No longer would the synagogue have been open to him, but once his message gained a foothold, the further it could advance. The report of it spread out over the flat country-side. The Jews could not abide these successes any longer. They managed to incriminate Paul and Barnabas in the eyes of the authorities, at the same time making use of the influence of the leading women proselytes; in fact they brought about the expulsion of Paul and Barnabas from the precincts of the city. It would have been possible for them to proceed westwards to Ephesus through Apamea; instead they turned eastwards. They obviously treated the plateau there as a unified missionary area. After a three or four day march over immense steppes they reached Iconium, a city which had achieved its importance as the centre of various roads which intersected at this point. The same spectacle occurred here as in Antioch. The preaching of the Apostle in the synagogue again provoked a division of opinion. The Jews appeared once more as the real opponents of Paul and only through timely flight did the apostles escape being maltreated and stoned. This time they turned south-east to the barren region of Lycaonia, where Cicero once took the field against robber bands. Augustus later planted a number of military colonies there, the indigenous population being severely cut off from this army of occupation. As a result the native Anatolian dialect had been preserved; Greek was understood only in the cities. All sorts of legends and superstitions survived here from ancient times. There were only a few Jews in this remote region. The apostles halted first in the little country town of Lystra, about twenty-three miles from Iconium. Today its position cannot be established with any certainty, but thanks to Acts this place will be spoken of for all time, because it has preserved for us a story which bears the stamp of truth simply on account of its local colour, however strange the details of it may seem to the modern man of intellect. The reader must look it up in Acts for himself (Acts xiv.8-20), if he is to feel the full effect of it. The healing of the cripple has its counterpart in the healing of the cripple by Peter at the Beautiful Gate (Acts iii). The effect upon the people of Lystra is religio-historically and psychologically quite credible. This region is the setting for the poignantly beautiful legend of the visit of Zeus and Hermes to the lovable old couple, Philemon and Baucis. The people of Lystra would certainly have been very familiar with it. They now believed themselves to be honoured with just such a visitation of the gods. The fact that they took Barnabas for Zeus and Paul, the spokesman, for Hermes, is highly significant; in fact we might characterise the relationship of the two men in these terms. The natives' discussions as to what they should now do were carried on in Lycaonian, which meant, of course, that their project took the apostles completely by surprise. For them this was not a case of pardonable superstition; as born Jews they had been trained in strict monotheism, a heritage of the Old Testament which Christianity rightly preserved. To the apostles, deification of man was a Gentile abomination. Nor did they wish to be mistaken for ancient miracle-workers such as were accorded divine honours in various places at just that time. Indeed, they sought not their own glory but that of Him who had sent them. It would have been difficult enough for them to make that fact clear to the excited crowd of people. And yet God, the Creator of heaven and earth, was not unknown even to the Gentiles. He had certainly testified to them of Himself in nature and in their own lives and from Him came everything that filled their lives. In its outlines the speech at Lystra recalls the richer and more extended speech that Paul made on the Areopagus in Athens (Acts xvii.22-31). It is unlikely that Paul actually delivered it thus word for word. But it is certainly in accordance with the historical fact that Paul had to address the Gentiles in different terms from those in which he addressed the Jews in the synagogue. An immediate Messianic proclamation would have been completely out of place here. The audience would at best have confused Christ with one of the many divine figures of antiquity. Before Christ could be preached to the Gentiles they had to be led from polytheism to perception of the one true God who was exalted high above all human thoughts. The

first commandment would therefore have played a greater part
here than we might at first assume from his letters. The fact
that in the process Paul would have linked on to the Gentiles'
natural perception of God is supported by the testimony of the
Epistle to the Romans. It was the Gentiles' own fault if they no
longer clearly recognised the true divinity of God from the
works of creation (Rom. 1.19ff.), and even the Gentiles could
discern God's will in the voice of conscience (Rom. 11.14f.)
Every missionary must, of course, fasten on to what is already
available in the way of religious understanding in his hearers,
though, to be sure, not without clarifying and radically trans-
forming it. Paul would not have acted any differently. But,
having done that, he was assuredly impelled to reach his real
objective, the message of Christ, as quickly as possible. At the
same time, the reference to the imminent last judgment would
have played no small part (cf. 1 Thess. 1.9f., Rom. 1.18, 11.16).
From belief in the Creator to the proclamation of repentance,
judgment and the return of Christ—that is the steep curve in
which the Areopagus speech ascends, and these ideas are also
echoed in the speech at Lystra (Acts xiv.16). Even if Luke was
responsible for the composition of these speeches, they nevertheless reflect in their main features the manner in which Paul
actually did speak to the Gentiles.

The enthusiasm of the mob sometimes changes into the
direct opposite. That was what Paul and Barnabas had to
experience in Lystra. Jews from Iconium and Antioch succeeded in inciting the population to turn against the apostles.
Disappointment over the fact that the divine visitation which
they had thought to be real had already turned out to be an
illusion may have made their inflammatory work among the
people easier. Stones were hurled at Paul and he was dragged
out of the city half-dead (11 Cor. xi.25). The very next day he
left the city in company with Barnabas and made for Derbe.
It was there that he perhaps won for Christ, amongst others,
the Gaius mentioned in Acts xx.4. Paul did not wish to press
any further beyond this remote frontier city. His mission area
was the Graeco-Roman world. The journey home would have
led him in a few days over the Taurus to Tarsus; but he preferred on his way back to visit the newly founded churches once
more. He had left them for the most part as young infants.

They were born amidst manifold sufferings, and who knew what history of suffering awaited them yet? It was important, then, to strengthen, comfort and establish them (Acts xiv.22f.) When the apostles, after an absence of several years, arrived again at the church in Antioch, they could truly recount the mighty deeds of God which had occurred through them.

# THE APOSTOLIC COUNCIL
## AT JERUSALEM

THERE was no rest for an apostle, as Paul was to discover on his return to Antioch. New difficulties arose that were no less hazardous for Paul's work than the sufferings and hardship that he had just undergone. Here indeed was a matter of life and death for the mission to the Gentiles.

We saw earlier that after the death of Stephen a conservative element gained the upper hand in the mother church at Jerusalem. This fact had already found expression in the election of James as leader of the church. Christianity could not here be imagined as anything but a Jewish sect. Indeed, hitherto it had been believed that the Messiah had been promised to the Jewish people alone. Membership of the "chosen people" was thus the preliminary condition for a share in the salvation that the Messiah bestowed. If a man did not belong to this people by birth, he must at least join it by assuming the whole of the Law and circumcision in particular. Just as the Jewish Christians faithfully observed the precepts of the Law, so they demanded the same of the Gentile Christians. They simply could not conceive of another type of Christianity free from Jewish legal limitations. That meant, to put it in a nutshell, that the man who decided to become a Christian had first to become a Jew. Antiquated though this attitude may be in the light of later historical developments, we cannot blame these Jewish Christians for it. New movements in history seldom succeed at once; for the most part they have to be fought for violently.

Paul was destined to lead the struggle for the freedom of the Gospel from Jewish legalism. His forerunners in the struggle were the "Hellenists," Stephen and his partisans; but the chief responsibility for the decision fell upon him.

When the men of Cyprus and Cyrene founded the first Gentile Christian church in Antioch, the only hallmark of membership of the church was faith in Jesus Christ. Paul had not considered it otherwise on his first missionary journey. Was

63

that merely clever politics on his part? Did he wish to make it easier for the Gentiles than did the Jewish mission, in order to enter into successful competition with them? For one thing is quite clear: the requirement of circumcision was, for most non-Jews, an insuperable barrier. The Jew was not generally held in high esteem in those days (cf. Jn. xviii.35). To profess this people's religion in any way was, on obvious grounds, hardly possible for, say, the Roman official. Amongst the Gentiles who had embraced the Jewish religion there were on that account many more half-proselytes, the so-called God-fearers, than full proselytes who had assumed the whole of the Law. It is evident that Paul, with his unlegalistic preaching, had far greater prospects in these circles. For that reason he appeared to the Jews as an unfair competitor and was pursued by them with a deadly hatred. To Jewish missionary propaganda Paul seemed to be appropriating for his own ends the fruits of their unsparing labours (Mt. xxiii.15). One might indeed be inclined to speak here of clever politics. Never would Paul have become the Apostle of the nations had he imposed the Law upon the Gentiles. Never would Christianity have become a world-religion had it not burst the Jewish barriers. And yet it would be a quite superficial interpretation of the Pauline mission to ascribe its freedom from the Law to shrewd calculations and clever politics. The true reason is to be seen in the spiritual road along which Paul was led in his development from a Pharisee to an apostle. Because he had been certain since the hour of his conversion that Christ was the end of the Law, he was able, indeed he was obliged, to preach to the Gentiles an unlegalistic Gospel. Paul's missionary practice was rooted in the deepest insights bestowed upon him by his encounter with Christ, and owed nothing to opportunism. Truly the man who in a very critical hour of his life wrote the words in Gal. i.10 has nothing in common with opportunism. But well may the Apostle on occasion have suspected dimly that he had here ventured a step which would yet lead to clashes. Perhaps it was with this secret care in his heart that he left the city after his visit to the leaders of the mother church. Now was the hour in which the decision had to be made.

The immediate occasion was provided by the disquiet let loose in the church at Antioch by certain representatives of the mother church. According to Acts xv.5 it had to do with people who before their conversion to Christianity had belonged to the sect of the Pharisees. They had evidently come to see the situation in Antioch at close hand (cf. Gal. ii.4). What they observed there aroused their sternest disapproval. No validity was attached here to food-commandments, purity-regulations and other Jewish laws. In their indignation they refused to sit at the Lord's Table with such "co-believers." They regarded with horror the freedom with which Paul and Barnabas consorted with these Gentile Christians. Could what confronted them be called Christianity at all? Only a radical change of attitude would suffice in this case: the Law had to be assumed unconditionally. "Unless you are circumcised according to the custom of Moses, you cannot be saved" (Acts xv.1). One can imagine the uproar that this demand created in the church at Antioch. Could their road so far have been really so mistaken? Why had they not been told this earlier? And what was the situation regarding the authority of their honoured leaders, Paul and Barnabas? Were they somehow in opposition to the celebrated first apostles in Jerusalem? On what side, then, had they to range themselves? The Antiochenes did not know what to do. To become Jews was impossible; still less could they give up their Christianity.

Paul was not for one moment in doubt regarding the correctness of his course so far. Christianity and the Law was for him more than just a question of how the Law could be modified so as to enable Gentiles to accept it and thus be received into the Church. For him it was based totally upon his experience of salvation. It was precisely for that reason that he could not and would not give way in this matter (Gal. i.8), and here the authority of the first apostles and the mother church was not decisive for him. He considered that his own apostolate was in no way inferior to that of those who were apostles before him (Gal. ii.6). And in that respect Paul was surrendering to no self-deception: he had thought and agonised (Gal. ii.19) through the question of "Law and Gospel" more than the men of the mother church. One thing was quite clear to him: a reversion from unlegalistic to legalistic Christianity would be a falling-away from Christ (Gal. v.4). One might even say that for Paul it was not so much a matter of Church politics as of dogma, though here we must not interpret the word "dogma" in a narrow pedantic sense. A vital issue was at stake.

Personally, therefore, Paul was completely sure of his cause. Why did he nevertheless appeal for a decision from the mother church? On this point, we can only hazard guesses, based upon conclusions drawn from other observations regarding Paul. He would have brought about the decision in Jerusalem out of consideration for the church in Antioch. We know from 1 Corinthians how vehemently Paul refused to tie a church to his person. The churches belonged to Christ, not to any religious leader. The apostolic authority was delegated authority. Personal though the relationship between apostle and church might be, this relationship was not compatible with the "cult of personality." It was this danger which had to be avoided in the case of Antioch. In any dispute with Jerusalem Paul would presumably have enjoyed and retained the support of the church in Antioch. But it was just this situation which appeared dangerous to him. The Antiochenes and all the other Gentile mission-churches were not to be Paulinists but simply Christians. For that reason Paul strove for the agreement of Jerusalem. But it mattered even more to Paul that the two sections of the early Church, Gentile Christians and Jewish Christians, should not separate. The fact that Paul fought for this unity with the full weight of his personality is perhaps the greatest service that he rendered to Christianity. We shall see later what the preservation of unity meant for both parties.

To secure the right decision in this important matter was Paul's greatest concern. In the light of this we can well understand the sentence: "I went up (to Jerusalem) by revelation" (Gal. ii.2). Nevertheless this resolve could have been at the same time in accordance with the wishes of the Antiochenes (Acts xv.2). We need not speak here of a contradiction in the two accounts. Only in Galatians (ii.1) is a certain Titus mentioned as one of the companions of Paul and Barnabas. Paul evidently took him as a sample of an uncircumcised Gentile Christian; we later come to know him as one of the most industrious of the Apostle's associates (ii Cor. vii.13ff.) This model disciple of Jesus, drawn from the ranks of the Gentiles, was intended, as it were, to be practical evidence for the vindication of unlegalistic Gentile Christianity.

The descriptions of the negotiations in Jerusalem contained in the two accounts, Acts xv and Gal. ii, do not entirely agree. We can disregard unimportant details. The main difference lies in two directions: first, in the differing role that Paul plays in the negotiations, second, in the matter of the so-called "Apostolic Decree."

(1) According to Acts what sets the ball rolling is the renewed demand of the former Pharisees for the circumcision of the Gentile Christians. We shall have to think of them as the "false brethren" of Gal. ii.4. According to Galatians Paul himself appears to move the settling of the Law question (Gal. ii.2). Acts xv gives Peter the first word. He refers to the conversion of the Gentile Cornelius, which had taken place "in the early days" through him, in order to draw conclusions which could equally as well stand in Galatians (*e.g.* ii.16). This strikes us as remarkable in so far as, in Galatians, Peter hears as a reproach what he here puts forward as his own opinion. When Peter had spoken Paul and Barnabas were required to report upon their successes in the Gentile mission (Acts xv.12). This report would not have failed to impress their audience. But, for all that, the decision has not yet been reached. It can only come from the side which feels itself attacked by Pauline practice. They must have waited with bated breath for the word of James which brings the eagerly-awaited concession: the rule of circumcision is waived by the head of the Law-observing party. This represents an enormous victory for Paul, even in the Acts account. To be sure, it is here ascribed more to the good-will and insight of Peter and James than to the stormy insistence and greater impact of Paul. The latter, however, is the picture that results from Galatians ii. Here everything decisive proceeds from Paul. He speaks in almost contemptuous tones of those who were "of repute"; they have nothing to contribute to him. They have rather to acknowledge his successes and thereby endorse his practice. Peter and James in no way appear here as those who have a more authoritative word to utter; they have merely the opportunity of declaring themselves in agreement with Paul after the event. They agree, moreover, upon a division of labour: Paul and Barnabas go to the Gentiles; the original Apostles will from now on restrict themselves to the Jewish mission.

If we ask at this point which picture is more in accordance
with historical fact, we must undoubtedly give preference to the
account in Galatians, which stands closer to the event than
Acts. We see then—and this may be of some comfort to present-
day readers—that even primitive Christianity did not lack
sharp antitheses. In the second generation, to which Acts
belongs, these antitheses had already been resolved. Paul had
conquered, and thus even his struggle appears in a gentler
light. As a result, Peter himself is delineated in Pauline terms,
a procedure which is not in accordance with the historical facts.
Paul, on the other hand, assumes Petrine features which he did
not possess. They both approximate to the apostolic type as
seen by the second generation. The real historical situation was
more discordant but also livelier. We must in this instance
remind ourselves that the Bible is not primarily a history-book.
Its value is not diminished by the fact that in this case it is
subject to the laws of human comprehension.

(2) According to Acts xv.20 and 23ff., although circumcision
is certainly not demanded of the Gentile Christians, they are
to submit voluntarily to a few conditions for the sake of inter-
course with the Jewish Christians. The decision is conveyed to
them in writing (xv.29). This document is usually called the
"Apostolic Decree." A whole literature has already appeared
regarding this Apostolic Decree. We must give it at least a brief
glance.

The greatest difficulties have arisen from the fact that the
text of the decree has been transmitted in different forms. The
old manuscripts diverge considerably at this point, according
to whether they derive from the eastern or the western half of
the Roman Empire. The eastern tradition, upon which the
Authorised Version is based, enumerates four items from which
the Gentile Christians were to abstain: "meats offered to idols,"
"blood," "things strangled" and "fornication" (xv.29 A.V.) On
closer glance these are seen actually to comprise only three
items, for by "blood" and "things strangled" are meant the
same thing. We are clearly dealing here with a food-regulation.
The Jew was permitted by his Law to eat only "kosher," that
is "pure," food, which involved draining meat of its blood.
According to a primitive view (Lev. xvii.11), the life was contained in the blood. It was feared that by taking the blood one

would imbibe the soul of the animal. Hence arose the Jewish custom of ritual slaughter. The Gentile Christians had also to fall in with this custom; that is what the abstention from blood and things strangled signified. The refraining from "meats sacrificed to idols" is to be interpreted in a similar fashion. It had nothing to do with the fact, taken for granted, that sacrifice was forbidden to the Gentile Christians. The meaning becomes clear if we quote 1 Cor. x.25-31 by way of comparison. The meat of slaughtered animals which had not been used for the sacrifice was sold in the market-place. Because of the sacrificial ceremonies it had come into contact, as it were, with the pagan gods, and was thereby rendered unclean. It was from such meat that the Gentile Christians had to abstain. Probably this also implied staying away from pagan cult feasts (1 Cor. VIII.10, x.14ff.) Through such feasts men sought to unite themselves with the deity. If an invitation to a feast went out to a Christian he might not accept it even from social considerations. Finally, by "fornication" was meant the cult-prostitution so widespread at that time.

We see therefore that according to the eastern tradition we are dealing in the Apostolic Decree with ritual and cult precepts, food-commandments and cult ceremonies. We gain an entirely different impression from the western tradition. The abstention from "things strangled" is here omitted and the so-called "golden rule" substituted: "Do not do to others what you would not like done to yourselves." What is the significance of this alteration? The addition of the golden rule indicated that the Apostolic Decree is here to be understood as a kind of ethical code. By cancelling the reference to "things strangled" it is possible to interpret the prohibitions ethically. By "blood" is meant murder, then, and no longer the blood of non-ritually slaughtered animals. The refraining from sacrifice to idols, murder and fornication represented the minimum ethical demand that could be imposed upon the Gentile Christians. These later became the three "deadly sins" which involved exclusion from the Church.

Which text may we assume to be the original, the eastern or the western tradition? Arguments have been advanced by noted authorities on both sides. Yet the following consideration is surely in decisive support of the eastern tradition. We

can well understand how, in an age which knew no problem of
Jewish and Gentile Christianity, ritual precepts with a ritual
origin were changed into ethical. On the other hand, the
opposite process would be scarcely conceivable. There is also
a second factor. Assuming that the Apostolic Decree really did
consist of ethical precepts, they would nevertheless have been
completely inadequate. Would it really have been necessary
first to impress upon the Gentile Christians, won for Christ by
Paul's preaching, that they should abstain from murder? Such
self-evident matters could have been left unsaid. Because that
was obviously felt to be the case with the western tradition, the
golden rule was added. We assume therefore that the eastern
tradition, according to which the Apostolic Decree comprised
food-commandments and cult-regulations, is the original.

But now arises a second question. Was the Apostolic Decree
promulgated at all at that time? We must answer in the
negative. The account in Acts is at this point historically
inaccurate. There are three grounds for this verdict:

(1) The account in Galatians knows nothing of such conditions. The only reference here is to a division of the mission
area, besides which Paul and Barnabas give an undertaking
to remember the poor of the mother church. Paul did indeed
raise these collections for Jerusalem (Rom. xv.1, 1 Cor. xvi,
ii Cor. viii and ix, Acts xx.16ff.)

(2) On the other hand we have no evidence that Paul in his
later missionary work abided by, or invoked the precepts of,
the Apostolic Decree. He would have had occasion to do so
during the course of his argument in 1 Corinthians (viii.4-10,
x.25-31), but we hear no mention of the Apostolic Decree.
Paul leaves it rather to the conscience of the individual and
merely recommends consideration for the weak. But we must
not assume that Paul disregarded the Jerusalem conditions,
for the more feasible conclusion is that he had no knowledge
of them at all.

(3) A narrative in Acts itself stands in agreement with this.
When Paul arrives in Jerusalem for the last time he is informed,
by James and the elders, of the contents of the Apostolic Decree
as though they were news to him (Acts xxi.25). As Acts therefore contradicts itself on this point, we have all the more reason
to abide by the Pauline account, according to which the

Apostolic Decree was not agreed upon at the Jerusalem Council, but only settled later. The occasion was perhaps provided by the discussion of Peter and Paul in Antioch (Gal. II.11-21).

The Jerusalem decision was an unqualified success for Paul. We must not, of course, overlook the fact that the first Apostles also rose nobly to the occasion. They would have been justified in thinking that it was up to Paul to give way. He had joined the Church later than they, and might have fallen in with them, who were indeed "of repute." But they did not stubbornly abide by their former views. All honour to the Apostles for the fact that, selflessly and ungrudgingly, they acknowledged Paul's mighty work and yielded to his demands for the sake of the common cause. But the chief credit for this decision lies nevertheless with Paul. The significance of this hour is twofold. The dropping of the legal requirement opened up the way for Christianity to become a world religion. Without Paul Christianity would have become a Jewish sect, and probably it would then have been involved in the political destruction of Judaism. In actual fact, Jewish Christianity no longer played any great historical role. But that is only one side of the affair. Paul also applied all his energies to ensuring that early Gentile Christianity did not lose touch with the mother church. In this way he rendered a tremendous service to Gentile Christianity; for it owed two things to its connexion with the mother church: the Old Testament and the Gospels, both of which kept Gentile Christianity from perishing under the syncretism of the ancient world (*i.e.* the intermingling of different religions). From the Old Testament they acquired a strict, unrelenting monotheism, in addition to which they had the information concerning the actual life of the historical Jesus. Without the Old Testament with its monotheism and without the tradition of the historical Jesus, the person of Christ would have degenerated, in the eyes of the Gentile Christians, into one of the many gods which comprised the pantheon of those days. Christianity would have become, in the process, a pagan sect. That it became neither a pagan nor a Jewish sect but a world religion is due to the bold and far-seeing attitude of Paul. In this fact lies the deepest significance of the Apostolic Council at Jerusalem.

F

# THE SECOND MISSIONARY JOURNEY

AFTER the Jerusalem decision had been reached Paul and Barnabas returned to Antioch. Acts has nothing in particular to say about this stay (xv.35). On the other hand we must presumably insert at this point the event that Paul relates in Gal. ii.11-21. The Lord's Supper was then linked with a common meal, the so-called "love-feast" (*agape*). In Antioch this love-feast gave rise to table fellowship between Gentile Christians and Jewish Christians, who were evidently very much in the minority, without any adherence to the Jewish food-regulations. Pauline freedom prevailed here, and no one made any objection. When Peter visited Antioch he entered into this fellowship without hesitation. The situation altered when certain men arrived from James. This table fellowship appeared intolerable to them despite the Jerusalem settlement. Peter himself then became alarmed at his own temerity; he withdrew, and the rest of the Jewish Christians there took fright with him. Even Paul's old companion, Barnabas, wavered. We see how difficult it is to rid oneself of the old prejudices; fear of public opinion may also have played a part. Paul described this aloofness, with no beating about the bush, as hypocrisy. He did not hesitate to call Peter to account before the assembled church. In plain words, he branded his actions as false and of soul-imperilling inconsistency. Paul tells us nothing of the outcome of the discussion. We may well assume, however, that, as in Jerusalem, so in Antioch, Paul proved himself the stronger.

This story was extremely painful to the older Catholic expositors: it does indeed appear to do extreme damage to the authority of the "Prince of Apostles," the first "Vicar of Christ." Luther, on the other hand, invoked this story, not without reason, in his struggle against the Papacy. It teaches at all events what many a Catholic exposition admits today: even the apostles were human. Certainly they were selected by God for a special ministry; such was the basis of their dignity. But, for all that, they remained men who had their weaknesses and their weak moments. What we have to say here about Peter, whose impulsive manner once again caused his downfall, applies on other occasions even to Paul. The authority of the apostles rested not upon their apostolic privilege but was valid only in so far as they discharged their commission.

It could not have been easy for Paul to stand against Peter in this way. He made this sacrifice for the sake of the cause. Personal considerations could not be finally decisive where the Gospel was concerned. The bitter realisation of this fact was perhaps one of the most intimate sorrows of Paul's apostleship. It was brought home to him once again after his encounter with Peter. Paul was once more drawn towards missionary work, and his thoughts dwelt on the newly-founded churches of Asia Minor. Were they not in urgent need of his personal support? The question left him no peace; he could not remain in Antioch any longer. But his plans extended still further. In many regions of the mighty Roman Empire no news of Jesus Christ had as yet penetrated at all. It was important to conquer these regions for Christ. This was the goal which would not let Paul rest. He submitted his plans to Barnabas, his faithful travelling companion, but this now led to a rather painful separation. Barnabas would not move without taking his cousin Mark along with him as his companion. Paul would not agree to this at all. Mark had failed the test once before; Paul did not want to give him a second trial. Barnabas was thinking of the person, Paul of the cause. Barnabas was lenient in his judgment, Paul, like many great men, harsh and unyielding. He imposed upon others the standards by which he himself lived. We can understand both Paul and Barnabas; but they, at this moment, could not understand each other. It was perhaps not only the person of Mark, but also the question of the journey's destination that caused the "contention" (Acts xv.39) between the two men. Be that as it may, it came to a separation. An alliance that had held firm in various ways both in good times and in bad broke up then. From a human point of view it was deeply regrettable. But for the extension of Christianity it was probably an advantage. The two apostles could go their separate ways and yet march in step. That the dispute did not lead to any lasting enmity is shown by the acknowledgement of Barnabas in i Cor. ix.6. The unifying bond of obedience to Christ proved stronger in the long run than the personal difference of opinion.

So Barnabas returned to Cyprus with Mark. Paul, however, found a new companion in Silas. Silas had been a leading man in the mother church (Acts xv.22). As such he was chosen with one other to convey the Apostolic Decree to the church in Antioch. He evidently felt himself at home there; according to a reading adopted by the Authorised Version he remained there (Acts xv.34). We do not know how long he had possessed Roman citizenship (Acts xvi.37). The fact that he bore a dual name has perhaps some connexion with this; the Latinised form "Silvanus" stands alongside the Semitic "Silas" (1 Thess. 1.1, ii Thess. 1.1). As a member of the mother church Silas had connexions with Peter which emerge later on (1 Pet. v.12). So Silas was very well qualified outwardly to accompany Paul; that he was inwardly well-qualified too is shown by the statement (Acts xv.32) that Silas was a prophet. By this was understood in the New Testament period a man whose preaching was based on personal revelation (1 Cor. xiv.29ff.)

Paul set off with this man on his journey. This time he did not go by sea but went by way of Syria and Cilicia. The district was familiar to him from an earlier occasion (Gal. 1.21), partly, indeed, from boyhood. There was also no lack of Christian churches there who would have welcomed a visit from Paul. From Tarsus the route led over the Cilician Taurus to Lycaonia and the already familiar Derbe and Lystra (Acts xiv.6ff.) It was even more arduous and dangerous than the crossing of the Taurus from Pamphylia that Paul had ventured upon on the first missionary journey. It was along the same road that German Crusaders later bore the body of Barbarossa. Paul and Silas must have been glad and thankful when, after a march lasting several days, they saw the little town of Derbe lying before them. We can easily imagine the joy with which the church there greeted them, but Acts is silent on this point as on so much that we would like to hear.

The same applies to the stay in Lystra. Only one consequence of the activity there is mentioned, but it is admittedly a very important one: the winning of Paul's most faithful disciple, Timothy (Acts xvi.1-3). Nothing is known about him except that he was the son of a mixed marriage, and that his father was a Greek. In Greek "Timotheos" means "God-fearing": perhaps he had attended the Jewish synagogue as a "God-fearer." His mother is described as a "Jewish woman who was a believer." She would probably have joined the Christian Church on the occasion of Paul's first visit to Lystra. According to II Tim. 1.5 she was called Eunice and his grandmother, Lois. We may well assume that the boy had received a godly upbringing. According to II Tim. III.15 he was familiar with the Holy Scriptures from his childhood. On the other hand he did not belong in every respect to the Jewish community. As the son of a Greek father he was not circumcised, but before Paul received him into his service he repaired this omission. We may perhaps wonder greatly at this. What made Paul do it? Had he not just conquered in the struggle for an unlegalistic Christianity? Was not Titus also uncircumcised? Could even Paul then be inconsistent? On the basis of such considerations men have tried to prove that the account in Acts is fictitious. This, however, is completely unwarranted, for the two cases of Titus and Timothy are entirely different. In Titus's case it concerned a decision of principle upon which Paul could not give way. In the case of Timothy, however, practical considerations were decisive for Paul. On his travels Paul, as we know, always sought out the synagogues first. His activity among the Jews would have been needlessly handicapped if he had had an uncircumcised man with him. In his own mind Paul adopted a completely free attitude towards the question of circumcision; "for neither circumcision counts for anything, nor uncircumcision, but a new creation" (Gal. VI.15). For that reason, however, Paul could be not only a Greek to the Greeks, but also a Jew to the Jews (1 Cor. IX. 20ff.) Henceforward we see Timothy constantly in the company of Paul. To no other fellow-worker of his did Paul give a finer testimonial than to him: "I have no one like him, who will be genuinely anxious for your welfare. They all look after their own interests, not those of Jesus Christ. But Timothy's worth you know, how as a son with a father he has served with me in the gospel" (Phil. II.20-22).

The stay in Derbe and Lystra would not have lasted long. Of the next stage of the journey Acts XVI. 6-8 gives the following remarkable account: "And they went through the region of

Phrygia and Galatia, having been forbidden by the Holy Spirit
to speak the word in Asia. And when they had come opposite
Mysia, they attempted to go into Bithynia, but the spirit of
Jesus did not allow them; so, passing by Mysia, they went down
to Troas." If we trace this journey on the map we are struck
by the remarkably zigzag line which results. We must say,
here and now, that much of the account is incomprehensible
to us, but nevertheless, let us look a little at the separate halts.

We are not told whether Paul preached in Phrygia, the
province in the centre of Asia Minor. In later missionary
history its cities of Hierapolis and Laodicea were centres of
Christianity (Col. iv.13). Paul's objective was "Asia," by
which is understood the Roman province of "Asia" in western
Asia Minor, to which belonged the provinces of Mysia, Lydia,
Caria and Phrygia. This was the most Hellenised part of Asia
Minor. Here also were the great cities of Pergamum, Ephesus,
Smyrna and Sardis, among others, which vied with each other
for the pre-eminence. It was no wonder that Paul, who preferred the big city for his missionary work, was drawn in this
direction. But, according to the account in Acts, the Holy
Spirit forbade him. Paul undoubtedly allowed himself to be
directed very strongly in his missionary work by such higher
inspirations. We already saw this at the beginning of the first
missionary journey. Throughout his life Paul was guided by
"revelations." For him the Holy Spirit was no dogmatic concept or mere idea, but a highly concrete reality, of which he
was powerfully aware in his life. Even though such experiences
have become relatively foreign, we have no right to deny them
to Paul. Recent missionary history can tell of similar things.
If the modern historian were more familiar with the history of
missions, then much criticism which speaks in this instance of
an "impossible journey" would be silenced. Paul shows himself to be an "apostle," that is, "one sent," by the fact that he
did not decide his own line of march according to the map, but
allowed himself to be guided.

Paul turned, not westwards, but eastwards, into the "region
of Galatia." The region of Galatia is to be distinguished from
the province of Galatia. To the province of Galatia belonged
also the province of Lycaonia with the cities of Iconium, Lystra
and Derbe. The region of Galatia lay further north, to the

north-east of Phrygia. Its best known city was Ancyra (Ankara). The Galatians were racially foreigners in Asia Minor at that time. "Galatians" is the Greek name for Gauls or Celts. In the third century B.C. various Gaulish races from the region of Toulouse broke out towards the Balkans. They also invaded Greece. Eventually they settled in Asia Minor on both sides of the Halys. Hence the region was called Galatia.

Once again Acts is silent, in that it says nothing of Paul's stay there. Only from Galatians IV.13ff. can we conclude that he was stricken there with an illness. Perhaps this necessitated a longer stay and thus provided the outward occasion for the evangelisation of the area. We can only make conjectures regarding the nature of this illness. When Paul writes (Gal. IV.15) that the Galatians would have preferred to tear out their own eyes and give them to him, we must not on that account think immediately of an eye-disease. Paul's words could have been intended to mean, metaphorically, that the Galatians would have sacrificed their all for him. On the other hand, an eye-disease would fit in conveniently with the mention of Paul's temporary blindness after the Damascus experience. Anyway the Galatians received him with open arms, a fact that stirs us inwardly all the more in that, in the Galatians, we are not dealing with Asiatics, but with a people of Celtic stock, and therefore with heirs of our own Indo-European culture. Perhaps Paul came to understand then why the Spirit had led him into this remote region.

The account in Acts XVI.7 remains quite obscure. Even the many conjectures of learned research have been unable to throw any real light upon this matter. Troas, however, is named as the terminus of this strange zigzag journey through Asia Minor. The city lay not far from the ruins of ancient Troy. It had been built in honour of Alexander; and later Augustus had bestowed his favour upon it. It was a district full of great and proud traditions which bound Asia and Europe together. It was from there that a new bond was to be forged between the Orient and the Occident. The triumphal progress of the Gospel through Europe, more powerful and of greater consequence than that of Alexander, was to take its beginning from here. Acts XVI.9f. tells of a vision that came to Paul. Time and again he had the opportunity of gazing at merchants and

seamen from Macedonia in their national dress. The idea of
bringing the Gospel over to them may have frequently stirred
him. Perhaps Rome was even then the secret goal of his desires.
Paul's famous vision of the Macedonian beseeching him to
"come over and help us" caused the resolve to ripen into action.
God's command brooked no delay (Acts xvi.10 "immediately").
The consequences of this step were immeasurable. The destiny
of Europe was decided in that hour.

By the time Paul had reached the European coast by ship a
new comrade had joined him who was henceforward to remain
his faithful companion, namely, Luke the physician (Col. iv.14).
Nothing certain is known of his origin, though, according to a
tradition of the early Church, he hailed from Antioch in Syria.
He must at any rate be counted as a Gentile Christian. His
greatest achievements were the compilation of the Third Gospel
and of Acts. The Third Gospel bears clear traces of having been
written by a pupil of the great apostle to the Gentiles, for Luke
emphasises the same elements in the preaching of Jesus as
became most important for Paul. God loves the sinner who
repents more than the ninety-nine righteous persons who need
no repentance. Tax-collectors, sinners and Samaritans, the
beggars on the highways and in the hedgerows inherit the
Kingdom of God, while it remains closed to the Jews, to whom
it was promised. These are exactly the ideas which constitute
the Pauline message. In Acts, however, Luke has preserved for
us valuable material from the life of his master. Without it we
would not, in spite of the letters, have any conception at all of
the Apostle's life. This fact should not be forgotten by the all-
too pedantic critics of Luke's historical account. Luke probably encountered Paul in Troas; for it is at this point that the
so-called "we-passages" begin, where Luke narrates in the first
person (Acts xvi.10-17, xx.5-15, xxi.1-18, xxvii.1, xxviii.16;
also xi.28, according to the western tradition). These passages
are concerned purely with accounts of travel, the simplest
explanation of which is still that we are dealing with entries in
Luke's personal diary inserted into the body of the narrative.

With the help of a favourable wind Paul and his partner
landed in only two days at Neapolis (Kavalla). For the first
time they stood on European soil. Neapolis was the one harbour
in the area; it also lay on the famous old military road, the

Via Egnatia, which linked Macedonia with Rome. Nine miles further inland lay Philippi. The city was named after Philip of Macedonia, the father of Alexander the Great. Here in 42 B.C. the deciding battle took place between Caesar's murderers and Antony and Octavian. To commemorate this event Augustus elevated it to the rank of a military colony with Italian urban rights and freedom from tax (Acts XVI.12). The city in Paul's day had therefore a predominantly Roman character, although the Macedonian influence was by no means negligible.

Acts relates the events in Philippi so vividly and in such detail (Acts XVI.12-40) that we need only resume them briefly here. Compared with Paul's experiences in other cities, the impression given by the stay in Philippi is at first almost idyllic. The Jewish community was not large; they did not possess their own synagogue but only a place of prayer. Paul began his activity there, and made his first conversion, on European soil, of a woman, namely, a purple-seller from Thyatira. The city lay in Asia Minor, in the province of Lydia, hence the woman's name. The devout Gentile developed into a zealous disciple of Jesus, and her Christianity bore all the marks of first love. It was perhaps already at this time that those men and women joined the Church of whom we hear later in Philippians: Euodia and Syntyche, Clement and Epaphroditus (Phil. II.25, IV.2f.) Difficulties first arose as the result of the healing of a soothsaying girl. We would describe her today as a kind of spiritualist medium. Her morbid gift proved very profitable to her masters, possibly a pagan priestly body. Paul had no respect at all for such occult practices. He only saw that the girl, a slave, was suffering under her talent, and therefore healed her. The ensuing treatment of Paul and Silas was totally illegal, though such things happened occasionally even in the constitutional state of Rome. Anti-Semitic feelings among the population may also have played a part. Paul and Silas who, as Roman citizens, could not be flogged, did not have a chance to speak. They found themselves thrown unexpectedly into the grim city-prison. The narrative which follows of the miraculous release of the apostles and the conversion of the jailer is too well known to need reproducing here. Earthquakes are not out of the ordinary in this region. Nevertheless, we can understand the fear of the jailer, who had to vouch for his prisoners with his life. But the most striking feature of the narrative is the bearing of Paul and Silas: "But about midnight Paul and Silas were praying and singing hymns to God" (Acts xvi.25). The conversion of the jailer was not based upon any deep insight but upon a sudden shock. Nevertheless it could have been genuine and borne fruit later. God permits men to approach Him along very different paths.

The fact that next day Paul and Silas insisted to the Roman authorities that their rights must be respected (Acts xvi.35ff.), may perhaps occasion surprise to many who conceive Christianity in terms of patient endurance. Should they not, in accordance with the precepts of the Sermon on the Mount, rather have accepted the injustice in silence? That would be a visionary conception of Christianity, as represented, for example, by the Russian author Tolstoy. As long as we live in the world as it is the Christian must insist that justice and order are not infringed. Where else shall the weak find protection? That is a sound Lutheran view for which we can invoke the example of the Lord Jesus Himself. When the servant of the High Priest struck Him without cause, He called him to account (Jn. xviii.22f.) On the other hand, the fact that the hour might come when we must tolerate injustice in the interests of our Christianity is likewise demonstrated by the life of the Lord Jesus, as by that of all His disciples.

Still suffering from the results of the ill-treatment undergone, Paul and Silas set off once again. After a march of several days by way of Amphipolis and Apollonia they reached Thessalonica (Acts xvii.1ff.), a distance of about ninety miles from Philippi. When we realise Paul's physical condition at this time, we can only wonder at what he was able to accomplish physically. It was the power of Christ's Spirit which wrested these achievements from his so often weary body.

Thessalonica (Salonika) was originally called Therme. Later its name was changed in honour of a sister of Alexander the Great. Under the Romans it became the capital of the province. As an important place of commerce, wonderfully situated on the gulf, it developed into a large town. This would be the reason why Paul chose it for his mission, as well as the fact that it contained a large Jewish community. As always, Paul used the synagogue service as a starting-point for his preaching. It did not lack success, though neither did it fail to stir up enmity on the part of the embittered Jews, who descended with a riotous mob on the house of Jason, with whom Paul had found lodging. Even though they were not able to seize the Apostle, his stay in Thessalonica did not last much longer. All too soon he had to break off the work he had so successfully begun. How many such sad moments there must have been in the Apostle's life!

Paul and Silas desired to remain in the neighbourhood, however, for this alone explains why they made their next destination the remote town of Beroea. Twice Paul attempted to return to Thessalonica (1 Thess. II.18), but in vain. To be sure, he was not idle in Beroea; his missionary successes came to the ears of the Jews in Thessalonica, and a campaign of provocation began. All his life Paul had to suffer from the activities of this pack of hounds. Philippi, Thessalonica and Beroea, Paul had to leave all these three centres of his work in Macedonia prematurely. According to Acts XVII.14 he left Silas and Timothy behind, which indicates that the persecution was mainly directed against him. Timothy must have followed him soon afterwards, for according to 1 Thess. III.1f. Paul sent him back to Thessalonica from Athens. It was with good news that Timothy returned to Paul, who meanwhile had travelled on to Corinth (Acts. XVIII.5). The work in Macedonia had not therefore been fruitless.

Paul was escorted to the coast by the brethren and from there he proceeded by ship to Athens. Paul in Athens! An inexhaustible theme for the creative imagination! Two worlds met at this point, both great and powerful, determining history right up to the present day. During their long joint history they have both attracted and repelled each other, and even today it is impossible to sum up the relationship of these two powers in a simple formula. In the world as we know it there has hardly been any spiritual phenomenon so intrinsically dynamic as this history. It began in the moment that Paul entered Athens. This first encounter contained the seeds of all that followed. It is not for nothing that Acts XVII gives the impression of being the climax of the whole book. It is as if the account itself were holding its breath. The description of this historical moment is in a form appropriate to its universal importance.

Athens at this time was only a shadow of its former greatness. In 146 B.C. Greece had become the Roman province of Achaia; vast tracts of territory were devastated. To take away a people's political freedom is to break its back; and such was the case with the Greeks of those days. They lived on the glory of their past, and that is never good for a nation. A nation lives not upon its past but upon its future. Athens was still certainly the "apple of Greece's eye," but nevertheless it had, to a great extent, declined into a museum. It is true that as an unequalled city of art it was invested with an imperishable glory. Ever since the conquering Romans had become subject to the superior culture of conquered Hellas, Athens had enjoyed a constant stream of Roman art enthusiasts and connoisseurs. Men such as Cicero, Ovid, Horace and Virgil had here received unforgettable impressions. Even today it is impossible for anyone who is not a complete philistine to remain unaffected by the overwhelming beauty of its classical monuments. To stand on the summit of the Acropolis and perceive the wonderful harmony of nature and art, of sun, sea and marble, is to see something that will be remembered for the rest of one's life.

Certainly Paul would not have walked blindly through all this beauty, yet he looked at the city through very different eyes from those of the modern worshipper of classical art. Aesthetic enjoyment presupposes an attitude of mind which is quite free from utilitarian thoughts and definite purposeful aims. But it was impossible for Paul to bring such a free and serene attitude to bear upon the treasures of Athens. For these works of art, for all that they possessed their own intrinsic validity, were not intended at that time for aesthetic enjoyment; rather, they served religious ends and were bound up with quite specific religious conceptions. For the men of that day Athens was not only the city of art but also, with its many holy places, the city of religion. Paul could not ignore these religious conceptions in order to surrender himself to the undisturbed enjoyment of art. For Paul, who had been trained from the beginning in image-free worship of God, this art was inescapably bound up with the pagan polytheism of antiquity. No sensible person could reproach him on that account, for we must not judge his attitude on the basis of modern preconceptions, which have no relevance to those days. Paul was shocked at the polytheism, and he had never seen so many images and effigies as he did in the city in which, according to an old saying, it was easier to meet a god than a man. We can thus understand the statement in Acts xvii.16: "Now while Paul was waiting for them (*i.e.* Silas and Timothy) at Athens, his spirit was provoked within him as he saw that the city was full of idols."

Paul visited the synagogue in Athens, but the Jewish community there was not numerous, and was also strongly secularised. More important were Paul's speeches in the marketplace, the *agora*. For the Athenians there was nothing out of the ordinary in the fact that speeches of a moral or religious content were delivered here. Many such itinerant preachers wandered at that time up and down the country in rough clothes, carrying a staff and pouch, barefoot and destitute, expounding their wisdom. The Athenians were all for anything new, however superficial, and they therefore gave Paul a hearing. We must not imagine the philosophers, the Epicureans and Stoics, who are mentioned as among his audience, to be great scholars or deep thinkers. They corresponded somewhat to the modern *littérateur*. Their chief skill lay in the clever draping of other people's ideas, and their philosophising was mainly a pose. Paul was contemptuously called a babbler (Acts xvii.18), literally "seed-picker." This was a favourite term of abuse in Athens at that time. Others took the matter more seriously, for Paul appeared to them to be preaching new gods. This recalls the famous charge levelled against Socrates, though it must not be interpreted here as a threat of legal proceedings. We must not think of the Areopagus as being the judicial authority known by that name; by it is probably meant the "Hill of Mars," which rises directly beside the Acropolis, and on which the criminal court used to sit in ancient times.

Paul's "Areopagus Speech" which now followed is one of the most impressive passages in Acts. We shall discuss its authenticity in a moment; first, we must acquaint ourselves with its contents. The speech begins with a certain recognition of pagan religiosity: the Athenians are extremely "religious." The expression is ambiguous; the Athenians could interpret it in their favour. Then follows the famous reference to the "unknown god." We have historical evidence only for altars with the inscription "to unknown gods," the motive being not to

overlook and thereby offend any of the unknown deities as well
as the familiar indigenous gods. We must probably attribute
the singular form to the Areopagus speech itself, which in this
way gains powerfully in depth and at the same time achieves
an ingenious point of contact. In fact, hidden under the
religious traffic of those days, with its polytheism, there was the
yearning after the unknown God, of whom the great minds of
Greece had spoken in sublime philosophical speculations.
Monotheism was not completely alien to the cultured Graeco-
Roman world; but it was impossible for reason and devout
feeling to press beyond the "unknown god." We are reminded
involuntarily of Faust's confession of faith: "Who can name
Him? I have no name for Him; feeling is everything." What
now follows are thoughts of the kind that were expounded at
the highest levels of current Stoic philosophy. Indeed we can
find parallels even in the wording itself. These conceptions
were, to be sure, partly familiar to later Judaism. God is
exalted high above all that is human, and therefore is not
limited to human worship. He is the One who is furthest away,
and yet also the closest, "for 'in him we live and move and have
our being'; as even some of your own poets have said, 'For we
are indeed his offspring' " (Acts xvii.28). The quotation is
from the famous "Hymn to Zeus" of Aratus (c. 310-240 B.C.),
who hailed from Cilicia, Paul's own country, and later lived
for many years in Athens. But the quotation was frequently
employed in later Greek literature. We need not assume,
therefore, that Paul himself read Aratus's *Phaenomena*—after all
not everyone who quotes a well-known line from Schiller
knows its exact origin and context. The words regarding the
unity of the human race (Acts xvii.26) correspond similarly to
views held by the Stoics of those days, but were probably not
palatable to the proud Athenian audience.

Up to this point (Acts xvii.29) the speech strives to create a
link with the religious and philosophical ideas of the higher
Hellenism. But now it makes a steep curve: though hitherto
it has been a time of ignorance, now men must repent, the
judgment is imminent, the decision as to life or death rests with
Jesus Christ. The theme of the Resurrection begins to sound
forth.

Can we regard the Areopagus speech as the reproduction of

a genuine speech of Paul's? We must presuppose, as a matter of course, that we are not dealing with a verbatim reproduction, for which it would obviously be too short. Reference has already been made to the borrowings from Stoicism. We cannot of course entirely rule out the possibility of such borrowings in the mouth of Paul, who hailed from the city of Athenodorus. He did indeed incorporate the Stoic concept of conscience in his own terminology. Why should not Paul here, as on other occasions, adapt himself as far as possible to the linguistic and intellectual conventions of his audience? The Areopagus speech contains no directly un-Pauline thought. Even in Romans Paul is able to evaluate paganism in positive terms, in spite of his utter rejection of it (Rom. 1.19ff., 11.14f.); on the other hand, the Areopagus speech does not keep silent regarding the judgment to which paganism's most devout yearning for God must be subjected. We need not suspect that the speech was borrowed from extra-biblical literature, particularly as in this case no one has succeeded in producing exact proof of such borrowing. Yet, even though we are not dealing with a verbatim speech of Paul's, neither are we confronted with a piece of invention on Luke's part. Paul would indeed have spoken in Athens in terms similar to those recorded here.

No great success attended the speech; the Athenians dismissed the Apostle with a courteous phrase. "So Paul went out from among them" (Acts XVII.33). In this pithy sentence we can detect the tread of world history. With Paul went Athens's future; in this hour of decision it finally became a city of the past. Not that the historic encounter between Christianity and Hellenism was at an end; on the contrary, it had only just begun. But the city of Athens no longer played any decisive role in this struggle. How very different in this respect was the fate of Rome, which, as the city of Peter and Paul, outlasted the changing times and became the "eternal city." Among the adherents whom Paul gained in Athens, two are mentioned (Acts XVII.34). A comprehensive literature later attached itself to the name of one of them, Dionysius the Areopagite. It concerned the mystical writings of an unknown Greek theologian of the sixth century, who was strongly Neoplatonic in outlook. For centuries the Apostle's disciple was venerated as the author of these writings. Only in modern times was the pseudonym recognised, although this in no way altered the significance of the writings in themselves.

Paul himself seems to have suffered from this failure in Athens. He writes to the Corinthians that he arrived "in weakness and in much fear and trembling" (1 Cor. 11.3). He probably feared that he would fare similarly in Corinth. Even the life of this strong man did not lack hours of despair.

It was not without reason that Paul chose Corinth as his next destination. Although it had been completely destroyed by the Romans on the overthrow of Greece, it was rebuilt under Julius Caesar and, thanks to its extremely favourable situation between two seas, it became the chief commercial city and capital of the province of Achaia. It was quite different in character from Athens. In contrast to the city of artistic and scientific tradition, quiet Athens, it was a noisy city of world commerce which lived completely in the present. In the nature of things it was impossible to sense in the motley population of Corinth any of the Athenians' pride in their lineage. The immorality which prevailed in Corinth was proverbial; this was connected not merely with the lively traffic of the seaport, but especially with the famous and notorious Temple of Aphrodite, which stood on the summit of the Acrocorinth, and where nearly a thousand prostitutes lured both natives and foreigners to physical and spiritual ruin. The man who led a dissolute life would be described as "playing the Corinthian," and there was a current saying to the effect that "it is not given to every man to journey to Corinth." Even though Oriental influences played their part in these phenomena—this Aphrodite bore resemblance to the Phoenician Astarte—we cannot close our eyes to these blots on ancient culture, and we can judge from this the significance which Paul's mission had in respect of morality.

Paul found lodging and work in Corinth with a Jewish couple named Aquila and Priscilla. They had both lately migrated from Rome during the persecution of Jews which took place under Claudius (A.D. 49). They were probably already Christians. Paul was able to practise his trade at their home and was thus relieved of the necessity of becoming a financial burden to the growing church in Corinth. This relationship developed into a lasting friendship which held firm later in Ephesus (Acts XVIII.2, 18, 26). This friendship would have been a particular source of refreshment to him after his experience in Athens. The return of Silas and Timothy (Acts xviii.5) also meant new encouragement for him. The conversion of the Gentiles was rich compensation for his rejection by the synagogue. In addition to Acts, both letters to the Corinthians give a list of names which are probably to be reckoned amongst the first-fruits of the Apostle's activity in Corinth. These letters give us, moreover, very interesting glimpses into the life of the Church there. Alongside much that was gratifying, there was no lack of dark corners, only too conceivable in a city like Corinth. We must beware of idealising early Christianity, for that would not be the Bible's intention. In any event there is hardly a Pauline church which we know so well as that in Corinth.

One episode, which fell probably at the end of the first visit to Corinth (Acts xviii.11f.), is of special interest to us on historical grounds. The Jews' indignation towards Paul ricocheted against the dignified calm of the procurator Gallio, and turned into a manifestation of Anti-Semitism on the part of the Corinthians. This Gallio is well known to us as the brother of the philosopher Seneca; his lovableness is emphasised frequently in accounts of him. We know from an inscription found in Delphi that Gallio was procurator of Achaia from A.D. 51 to A.D. 52. This date offers the surest starting-point for calculating the Pauline chronology. Paul would accordingly have arrived at Corinth in the new year of A.D. 50 and departed again in the autumn of A.D. 51; although, of course, much uncertainty still attaches to these calculations.

Paul's success in Corinth was as great as his success in Athens was small. The Greek metropolis had its church, and a band of faithful helpers had rallied round Paul. It is clear that Corinth, with its lively trade and traffic connexions, was soon to become a stronghold of Christianity. II Cor. speaks of Christians "in the whole of Achaia" (II Cor. 1.1), and in Rom. xvi.1 we hear of Phoebe, "a deaconess . . . at Cenchreae," which was one of the two ports of Corinth.

The churches of Achaia would certainly have still been in need of the Apostle's presence, but once the foundations had been laid he felt the urge to press on. His objective, which had already twice occurred to him, was Ephesus. This time Paul

G

chose the sea route, and Aquila and Priscilla accompanied him on the voyage in order to seek a new life at Ephesus. They embarked at Cenchreae. Acts xviii.18 reports the fulfilment there of a vow which, in view of the word-order in the Greek text, is more likely to relate to Aquila than to Paul. The man who made such a vow allowed his hair to grow until the vow had been redeemed (cf. Num. vi). We know nothing of the occasion for this; the brief reference indicates that even in Paul's circle many usages of the Jewish Law were still observed.

Why Paul accelerated his journey (Acts xviii.20) we cannot discover. We are merely told of a short and successful appearance in the synagogue at Ephesus, after which the journey continued through Caesarea to Jerusalem, to end at last in his beloved Antioch. Here again Acts has very little to say.

The so-called second missionary journey was thus at an end. Over what heights and through what depths it had led! Paul had completed a tremendous achievement, as we realise when we retrace the line of march on the map and recall its separate stages, which are now something more to us than mere names. Even Paul's opponents had to admit that he had "worked harder than any of them." The man who has eyes to see is summoned, in face of this achievement, to praise the "grace of God," which in Paul's case "was not in vain" (1 Cor. xv.10).

# THE THIRD MISSIONARY JOURNEY

P
AUL's "third missionary journey" must be printed in
inverted commas, for it concerns neither a continuous
journey with a definite route, nor, primarily, the evangelisation of newly opened-up areas. On this "journey" Paul had,
rather, a fixed headquarters, namely Ephesus, from which he
visited the surrounding region and the churches that he had
already founded in Asia Minor, Macedonia and Greece.

From Antioch his journey lay along the highway through
Cilicia to Galatia and Phrygia. We know from Galatians and
elsewhere how greatly these churches needed reinforcement by
the Apostle. Paul then entered Ephesus for the second time,
the city which was now for about three years to be the centre
of his activity, now reaching its climax.

Ephesus owed its significance to the famous temple of
Artemis, which in ancient times was accounted one of the Seven
Wonders of the World. It was originally a Phoenician foundation, and even in Paul's day the worship of Artemis bore
Oriental features, even though it did not assume such a crude
and sensual form as that of Aphrodite in Corinth. For a lengthy
period the settlement which had sprung up round the shrine
stood under Attic rule, and this gave rise to a lively connexion
with Greece. On the very night that Alexander the Great was
born the temple was set on fire by the visionary, Herostratus.
Alexander later rebuilt it. Modern excavations have given us
an idea of its extent. It was half as big again as Cologne
Cathedral—that is, about a hundred and sixty-five by three
hundred and forty feet. A double row of pillars about sixty
feet in height surrounded it on all sides. Innumerable votive
offerings were stored within it. Legend had it that the image
of Artemis, carved in wood, had fallen from heaven. The lower
part of the body was covered with charms, the head bore a
mural crown. The multiplicity of breasts indicates that in
Artemis we are dealing not so much with the Greek goddess of
hunting as with an Oriental fertility- and mother-goddess. The
religious transfiguration of motherhood is a primitive and often-

recurring need. But in Christianity this need has found a much more spiritualised expression in the veneration of the virgin mother of the God-Man. It is pleasantly symbolic of the history of religion, that it was in Ephesus itself, famous on account of its Artemis, that the dogma of the "God-bearer" was promulgated for the first time.

Another glory of Ephesus was the theatre, which originated in the Roman period, and was capable of holding nearly twenty-five thousand people. But it was to the temple, which attracted numerous pilgrims, that Ephesus owed its trade even in Paul's day, although the harbour facilities were unfavourable. Since 133 B.C. Ephesus had been the capital of the province of Asia, and the atmosphere there was propitious for the Caesar cult which was just beginning. It was left to German research to find in that area an inscription which extolled the emperor Augustus as saviour of the world. The world was lost but Augustus was born. All strife was at an end; peace and good-will reigned on earth. These joyful tidings (Greek: *evangelion*) marked the beginning of a new era. The reader will notice at once the almost word-for-word parallel that this *evangel* has in the Christmas message of the angels. A city of the Emperor cult, Artemis worship and of the widespread sorcery connected with it: such was the Ephesus to which Paul wished to carry the message of Christ. Surely an unparalleled act of courage! And yet in the following centuries this Ephesus became the metropolis of Christendom in Asia Minor.

On his arrival in Ephesus, Paul found Aquila and Priscilla already there. Here again the Apostle made use of the natural point of contact offered by the synagogue for preaching the Gospel, until the complete separation which came about after three months. Paul then transferred his preaching to the school of a certain Tyrannus, which he used out of lecture hours. This activity lasted for two years.

There is a remarkable story of Paul's encounter with the "disciples of John" (Acts XIX.1-7). We have evidence elsewhere for the existence of such followers of the Baptist in the apostolic period. The polemic of the prologue to John's Gospel (Jn. 1.6-9; cf. Jn. 1.19ff., III.27ff.) was aimed at them. It is also noteworthy that, according to a tradition of the early Church, John the Evangelist had, in his old age, worked in Ephesus.

An example of Ephesian magical practices, to which even the Jews there fell prey, is the strange episode of the sons of Sceva (Acts XIX.13-20). The account of the superstitious veneration of Paul (Acts XIX.11f.) also gives us a glimpse into the history of the ancient religions, which have not completely died out but have assumed Christian forms, as is exemplified by, amongst other things, the worship of the saints and the veneration of relics. But we may ask whether God would not, so to speak, smile just as much over many a highly spiritualised form of adoration as over these primitive expressions of a childlike devotion.

The activity of the Apostle did not confine itself to Ephesus. His heart was stirred with that "anxiety for all the churches" (II Cor. XI.28) which gave rise to his letters, those spiritually powerful documents which will survive through the centuries. In particular his thoughts were ranging across to Macedonia and Greece. But the task in Asia was still far too pressing. Meanwhile, therefore, he sent across Timothy and Erastus (Acts XIX.22, cf. Rom. XVI.23). At that time various of the other churches in Asia would have sprung up, some of which were to achieve great importance in subsequent Church history. From Revelation II and III we learn where the seven letters were addressed: besides Ephesus there were Smyrna, Pergamum, Thyatira, Sardis, Philadelphia and Laodicea. In Acts XX.5ff. we hear of a Christian church in Troas which Paul heartened by a visit. In the immediate neighbourhood of Ephesus lay Magnesia and Tralles, known to us from the letters of the martyr-bishop, Ignatius of Antioch (died between A.D. 110 and A.D. 117). The threefold constellation of Colossae, Laodicea and Hierapolis shines out at us from the letter to the Colossians (IV.12f.) It was here that Epaphras, described by Paul as a "beloved fellow servant" (Col. 1.7), prepared the soil. So Ephesus became, partly under Paul and partly soon afterwards, the centre of a whole ecclesiastical province in the most important and significant part of Asia Minor. We understand now why Ephesus had always been the goal of Paul's desires.

So Paul stood in Ephesus at the height of his career. Even here, of course, there was no lack of suffering and opposition. The account in Acts betrays many gaps. Paul himself writes to the Corinthians that "I fought with beasts at Ephesus"

(1 Cor. xv.32). This is hardly to be taken literally but it does hint at dangerous opposition (cf. 1 Cor. xvi.9). Perhaps 11 Cor. 1.8-11 relates also to experiences in Ephesus. Paul must have escaped death by the skin of his teeth; it was perhaps at that time that Aquila and Priscilla rescued him at the risk of their own lives (Rom. xvi.3f.) Luke makes no mention at all of this; and the "uproar" caused by Demetrius with which he concludes the description of Paul's stay in Ephesus (Acts xix.23-40) does not entirely fit in with these personal testimonies of the Apostle. For the rest, Luke proves himself here to be an excellent story-teller, not lacking in sense of humour. The narrative is also a masterpiece psychologically. How true to life it all is—the local patriotism of the Ephesians, the power of mass-suggestion, the demagogic influence of Demetrius who is able so cleverly to cover his business interests with the cloak of idealism and patriotism, and finally the calm superiority of the official who knew exactly how to deal with the population! So the whole commotion died down. Paul, however, seems to have left the city soon afterwards (Acts xx.1).

The difficulties in the Corinthian church may also have contributed to this decision, in fact they may already have compelled Paul to make a short visit to Achaia, during the course of his stay in Ephesus. For according to 11 Cor. xii.14 and xiii.1 Paul intended to visit Corinth for the third time, while according to 11 Cor. 11.1ff. the second visit had passed off very painfully. This second visit lay between the writing of 1 and 11 Corinthians; Paul must therefore have started out for Corinth from Ephesus. But it did not lead to the desired result; in fact Paul was most deeply insulted by a member of the church (11 Cor. 11.5, vii.12). After his return to Ephesus he decided to send Titus back to restore order (11 Cor. vii.13f.), and sent by him a very forthright letter, the so-called "tearful letter" (11 Cor. 11.3f.), which caused pain to the Corinthians but was very effective (11 Cor. vii.8ff.) This letter has not been preserved for us. Acts xx.1f. carries on from this point in the story. Paul set off after Titus, so disquieted was he by the affair. Despite great missionary successes in Troas (11 Cor. 11.12f.), about which Acts says nothing, he went on to meet Titus in Macedonia. On receiving good news from him there, Paul at once sent him back to Corinth in order that he should prepare for the collection planned for the church in Jerusalem (II Cor. VIII.16ff.) He took our II Corinthians with him as an accompanying letter. Paul travelled likewise to Corinth at a slower pace and remained there for three months (Acts xx.2f.) The composition of Romans falls in this period.

According to a remark made in this same letter (Rom. xv.19), Paul must have pressed on from Macedonia as far as Illyricum. From Corinth his plans extended even further westwards; he aimed to carry the Gospel to the utmost boundary of the ancient world, the "Pillars of Hercules," that is, to Spain. On the way there he desired to become acquainted with the church in Rome.

But first it was important that another task be fulfilled. Paul had made up his mind to take the offerings of the Greek churches to Jerusalem personally. He knew the dangers of this undertaking; he knew the hatred that his compatriots cherished towards the great apostate. How easily it could lead to clashes in the narrow streets of Jerusalem which would cost him his life! Paul knew no fear, but he possessed a sufficient sense of responsibility not to expose himself to danger un-necessarily. Why, then, did he not hand the collections over to one of his fellow-workers? Why did he make for Jerusalem himself in spite of being filled with premonitions of death? There is only one feasible explanation: the unity of Christen-dom mattered more to him than anything else. This unity was possible, however, only if the young Gentile Christian churches remained in touch with the mother church. We have already become acquainted with this point of view in regard to the "Apostolic Council." It was to this "togetherness" that the collections gave expression; and to show how greatly it mattered to him, Paul delivered them himself. This fact ought finally to silence the charge that Paul split Christendom into two camps.

Paul originally intended to go by the sea-route, but in order to avoid being ambushed by the Jews he changed his plan and went through Macedonia. The eastward-bound ships were probably carrying many Jewish festal pilgrims. Paul might well have heard of a plan to assassinate him on the voyage. So he took leave of his companions and headed with Luke ("we") towards Macedonia. It was intended that they should all meet again in Troas after the Days of the Unleavened Bread.

The journey now proceeded unrelentingly from place to place in the direction of Jerusalem. Luke has sketched some wonderful scenes of this journey, over all of which there hangs a restrained mood of farewell. On the Sunday Paul celebrated the Lord's Supper with the church in Troas for the last time before his departure (Acts xx.7ff.) It was growing late and Paul still had much upon his mind. The calm solemnity of the atmosphere was rudely dispelled by the fall of Eutychus, but restored by his miraculous recovery. It is questionable whether, in view of the echoes of 1 Kings xvii.21 (Elijah), we are to think in terms of an awakening from the dead. Luke, however, recounts the miracle with fine restraint.

One of the first halts on the sea voyage that followed was Miletus. Paul was hastening to reach Jerusalem by Pentecost, and so renounced a visit to Ephesus. He simply summoned the elders of the church to Miletus (Acts xx.17-38). In moving words he took leave of them and strengthened them for the difficult times ahead. He stopped again for some little time in Tyre, where the gentle love of the church was able to refresh him with peace and quiet (Acts xxi.3-6). In Caesarea Paul stayed at the house of Philip. He had formerly belonged, with Stephen, to the seven who had been nominated by the Jerusalem church (Acts vi.1ff.) and had soon afterwards converted the Ethiopian eunuch (Acts viii.26ff.) What a triumphal progress the Gospel had made since then! And that was all due in the main to the work of the man who at that time had been persecuting the Church! Soon he would himself become the prey of Jewish fanaticism. The prophet Agabus, whom Paul already knew from his days in Antioch (Acts xi.28), declared to him symbolically the fate which threatened him. But Paul allowed nothing more to hinder him. It was impossible to cover the distance from Caesarea to Jerusalem in one day; the reference to Mnason, with whom Paul lodged (Acts xxi.16), therefore probably suggests an intermediate halt. The reception in Jerusalem was at first friendly, but by the next day the clouds were already gathering. However, before we pursue these events further, we must take a look at the world disclosed to us in Paul's letters.

# I AND II THESSALONIANS

THE first letter to the Thessalonians is the earliest part of the New Testament, a fact which would hardly be guessed by the ordinary Bible reader who, in the process of thumbing through his New Testament, comes upon the letters to the Thessalonians in a somewhat obscure spot. He would assume rather that the separate writings of the New Testament arose in the order in which they now stand. But this applies neither to the Gospels nor to Paul's letters. In the earliest lists of the New Testament books, the Pauline letters are transmitted to us in varying order. Generally, however, they were arranged according to length. At the same time, this order corresponded principally with the importance of the letters and became generally established. But the chronological sequence is different, and, in all probability, is as follows: I and II Thessalonians, Galatians, I Corinthians, II Corinthians, Romans, Philippians, Colossians, Ephesians (?), Philemon, the Pastoral Epistles (?). These letters were collected early on in the churches, and such collections would already have existed by A.D. 100. Gradually, as these were joined on to the Gospels, our New Testament came into being. By A.D. 200 the New Testament as we know it existed in the large churches as a closed collection of recognised sacred writings. The Church's judgment wavered longest over the admissibility of Hebrews and Revelation. We call this process the "formation of the canon." A separate discipline of New Testament study, the history of the canon, has pursued these questions in many a learned study, and has provided us with insights into the growth of the New Testament which were not granted to our forefathers.

The greatest things often begin in silence. When Paul prepared in Corinth to write to the Thessalonians, he could not have suspected that in this way the New Testament, the most significant book in the world's literature, would begin. He had absolutely no literary aspirations; for him it was simply a heartfelt necessity that he should once again say a few words to this church. He had to leave it more hurriedly than he would have

95

liked. Already he had made two vain attempts to visit the church once more, probably from Beroea (1 Thess. 11.18). In Athens he could not bear to remain any longer without news from Thessalonica, and sent Timothy to them (1 Thess. 111.1f.) He was able to return with good news for Paul (1 Thess. 111.6), who meanwhile had travelled on to Corinth and had already been active there for some time (Acts xviii.1-5). 1 Thessalonians was written immediately after Timothy's return.

We are dealing here with a genuine letter, not a dogmatic treatise. Many distorted judgments of Paul's letters arose because this fact was not sufficiently appreciated. The Pauline letters are not theological dissertations but occasional letters, with the one possible exception of Romans. We must not therefore approach them with false presuppositions. They do not unfold a theological system, and to look for one is to invite disappointment. Neither are they model essays based upon scholastic rules. Although they have for the most part a clear sequence of thought, they place no value upon ingenious arrangement with headings and sub-headings. Above all, they are not, despite their often gripping eloquence, products of rhetorical art in the style of many an ancient discourse. Rather were they written from life for life in the current Greek vernacular. Much light is shed upon their style by the ancient "occasional letters" which were preserved for us in the desert sands of Egypt. Papyrus research has been able to make many a contribution to the understanding of Paul's letters. But this point of view which is, essentially, perfectly true, must not be taken too far. The Pauline letters are certainly genuine letters, yes, even occasional letters, but what letters they are! They stand alone in the literature of correspondence throughout the ages. At every point they proceed from life and come to grips with life; and yet they bring everything, even apparent trivialities, into the light of the ultimate. They speak of men and their needs and joys, and, at the same time, proclaim Christ who bestows both and liberates from both. They address themselves to a particular set of readers, and yet express truths which apply to all generations. They are wholly the expression of a strong individuality, and have, at the same time, a universal character. They do not set out to be theological dissertations, and yet they are crammed full with the profoundest thoughts, the interpretation of which has occupied theology for nearly two thousand years. They contain no system, and yet have the strongest inherent compactness of thought. They are not works of art, and yet they are anything but a string of unrelated thoughts arbitrarily arranged. They are testimonies to a genuine humanity, and, at the same time, revelations of a divine Spirit. Only when, in the reading of them, we sense the intertwining of both these things shall we perceive their uniqueness and greatness.

The following observations cannot offer a continous exposition of the letters, let alone exhaust their richness. They are intended merely to provide some modest and elementary aid towards understanding them.

I Thessalonians falls quite roughly into two parts, a retrospect (I-III), and a prospect (IV and V); a fact which at once demonstrates its genuine epistolary character. Indeed this division is reflected in some way or other in all the longer occasional letters. Of course, it is the manner in which this retrospect and prospect are carried out which once again demonstrates the special character of these writings.

Besides Paul, Silvanus (*i.e.* Silas) and Timothy are named as authors. That is due to the Apostle's modesty, for in reality Paul is the sole author; but, because the Thessalonians would have been gladdened by the mention of those fellow-workers of the Apostle with whom they were most familiar, it occurs here.

The ancient method of beginning a letter differed from ours. The introduction consisted of three parts. First, the writer announced himself, then followed the name of the addressee in the dative, and, finally, the formula of greeting. All the Pauline letters have this threefold division, although in individual cases there is no lack of addition and embellishment, as can be seen from the introduction to Romans in particular. For Paul made something special of this traditional scheme. The additions occasionally suggest an overture, echoing the themes of the whole work at the beginning. The Pauline formula of greeting is particularly characteristic, for it represents a unique combination of both the Hellenistic and Semitic greetings. The Greeks wished each other "joy," the Jews "peace" (*shalom, salem*). By means of a simple alteration in the word Paul changed the Hellenistic greeting into a wish for grace. This combination of the Hellenistic and Semitic greetings acts as a symbol, for by his labours Paul did indeed unite these two worlds in Christ.

With a single exception (Galatians) Paul always immediately follows the greeting with thanksgiving. Paul—a model of genuine pastoral care—is bound to his flock by gratitude and intercession. The rest of the first chapter looks back upon the blessed reception of the Gospel amongst the Thessalonians. The formula "faith, love, hope" (cf. 1 Cor. xiii.13) occurs here for the first time (1 Thess. 1.3). The church may be compared with a city that is set upon an hill and cannot be hidden (Mt. v.14). She has become an example to the churches in Macedonia and Achaia. She has not buried the Gospel but has herself gone over to proclaiming it, and in that way has made a name for herself far beyond the borders of Greece. Vss. 9 and 10 impress us as a summary of early Christian belief.

CH. II looks back upon Paul's activity in Thessalonica. Vss. 1-12 sound like a defence against attacks upon his work. We need not assume, however, that these attacks, which possibly emanated from the Jews in Thessalonica, had found soil in the church. This would not be in accordance with the good impression created by Timothy's preaching. So we can assume that Paul is taking precautions in advance. The objections against which he is defending himself were typical and would often recur. He also wishes perhaps to distinguish himself from a type of idle wandering preacher, not uncommon in those days, who tried to make a living by unscrupulous means. The passage gives a wonderful picture of Paul the pastor. What a tender heart this powerful fighter possessed! A comparison of this passage with the narrative in Acts xvii.1-9 is also instructive. Here, in 1 Thessalonians we have a supplement to Luke's account; there the events are seen from without, here from within.

In contrast to the kindly tones of the first half of CH. II, the second half betrays a note of harshness (vss. 13-16). The violent outburst against the Jews rests upon experiences undergone by both the Thessalonians and Paul himself. God's anger against this people has already become manifest. How, in face of these passages, Paul could be represented as a Jewish propagandist is beyond comprehension. To be sure, Paul had not come to terms intellectually with the Jewish problem, as can be seen from his wrestlings with it in Rom. IX-XI. No one can reproach him for being unable to cut himself off from his people with an easy heart.

With II.17 Paul suddenly adopts a new theme and a new tone. He also addresses the Thessalonians once again. Such sudden transitions have recently been made intelligible by being treated, quite rightly, as pauses in dictation. Like all ancient writers Paul mostly dictated his letters (cf. Rom. XVI.22). Whether it was that the amanuensis grew tired, or that Paul for some reason or other had to break off, hardly any of the letters, with the exception of the short letter to Philemon, would have been written down or dictated at one sitting. Today we can still detect the pauses in dictation with a fair degree of certainty.

As regards subject-matter, vss. 17-20 belong wholly to CH. III. Our present chapter-divisions do not always correspond to the divisions in subject-matter. Of course, Paul was no more responsible for them than he was for the verse-divisions; not even the Gospels were originally divided up in this way. Our present chapter divisions originated in the thirteenth century, and the verse divisions in the sixteenth (we know how cursorily the latter task was done), and though they are now an indispensable aid to Bible-reference, we must try not to be conscious of them, as on occasions they even distort the sense. Vss. 17-20 of CH. II already belong, therefore, from the point of view of content, to CH. III. They describe the circumstances and events connected with the mission of Timothy with which we are already familiar. Right through this description there runs the red thread of the Apostle's love for his Church.

Again we may assume a pause in dictation. CH. IV.1 marks the beginning of the second part of the letter. Retrospect now gives way to prospect. The motto of Paul's exhortations for the future runs: "Abound more and more" (IV.1 and 10 R.V.). Many temptations associated with their old pagan existence have still to be overcome (IV.3ff.) Here, as elsewhere, Paul speaks gravely of the fact that sex and money are the the root of most sin, for Paul does not consider himself too high-minded to mention these somewhat crude things. But regarding their "love of the brethren" (IV.9) Paul gives the Thessalonians a wonderful testimonial; only here again his warning applies: "Abound more and more." The admonitions to lead a quiet, industrious life hint at what in the second letter becomes the object of more extended discussion.

The early Christian churches lived in eager expectation of the return of Christ. When the Son of Man returned on the clouds of heaven in great power and glory, then they, as the Church of the final era, would enter with Him into His kingdom. They would not have to wait much longer for their salvation to draw near. In this hope they lived, in this hope they bore patiently and gladly the trials of this age, persecution, disgrace and scorn. We shall certainly be there when Christ sets up His Kingdom: this joyful assurance lifted them above all the calamities of the present. But now they were faced with something with which they could not come to terms, something which confused and disquieted their spirits. Some members of the church had died, and Christ had not yet appeared. What was to be the fate of those who had fallen asleep? Would they be excluded from the final glory because they had not experienced the Day of Christ? These were agonising questions for those who mourned the death of dear relatives. Paul had to give them a word of comfort (IV.13-18). We Christians are not like the pagans "who have no hope." The comfortless idea that death is the end of everything is out of the question where Christians are concerned. Paul is not thinking, however, of the "immortality of the soul" with which even the Greeks were familiar. Such a "disembodied" existence would not, in his opinion, be any real life at all. The biblical hope is centred not upon the immortality of the soul but upon the resurrection of the whole man. This hope is founded upon Easter.

> ". . . . . . could the Head
> Rise and leave its members dead?"[1]

The unity with Jesus Christ of the man who dies trusting in Him can no longer be dissolved by physical death, for he also has a share in Christ's Resurrection. His faith is pinned not upon One who is dead, but upon the Living One. When Christ returns, those who have fallen asleep in the Lord will be awakened first.

---

[1] *Jesu meine Zuversicht*, tr. Catherine Winkworth in the *Chorale-Book for England*, London 1863, No. 59, stanza 2.

Those who have yet to experience the Last Day will in this way have no unfair advantage over those who have already died. Then they will all be taken up into the air upon the clouds for their solemn meeting with the Lord. Their fellowship with Him will thenceforward last for ever.

We are dealing here with a passage from the Bible which clearly demonstrates the coalescing of conceptions of only temporary application with those of universal validity. The problem that agitated the Thessalonians is not a perennial one. No Christian church today could reasonably call this concern their own. We are not dealing with the general problem of the fate of the departed, though we are concerned with this problem also. It has much more to do with whether those who died before the return of Christ would be at a disadvantage compared with those who survived. This question presupposed expectation of the imminent end of the world, a presupposition which has been belied by the wellnigh two thousand years of Christianity's history. In many respects Paul's answer is also relevant only to these particular circumstances. He too reckons with this presupposition and is convinced that he, for his own part, will experience the return of Christ, a hope which he later abandoned (II Cor. v.1ff., Phil. 1.23). We today would be unlikely to share Paul's view that Christ would actually, physically, return to the earth (IV.16f.), though he intended his expressions of this hope to be taken quite literally. Yet how wonderfully the eternal Christian hope shines through these, as it were, "dated" conceptions! Christ never lets go of the man whom he has seized: "For I am Thine and Thou art mine; and death shall never part us" (Luther). And how modestly restrained, how free from all material considerations and how heartening is the final outlook: "So we shall always be with the Lord"! This passage, which at first strikes us as so strange, has therefore something valuable to say even to us. That is the way of the Apostle, to reveal behind every transitory veil an eternal world of meaning.

The early expectation of Christ's return had not made Christians into fanatics, as we see from the passage which follows (v.1-11). It is dominated by two injunctions: keep awake and be sober! As no one knows in advance what hour Christ will come and since every kind of pious curiosity on this score is forbidden, watchfulness is necessary. But drunkenness and intoxication are the antitheses of sobriety, and the time for drunken revelry is the night. Christians, however, live in the dawn-light of the Day of Christ. This is therefore the time to keep awake and be sober and to put on the spiritual armour (cf. Eph. VI.10ff.) Christianity is not something sentimental and vague, but is characterised by an attitude which is both vigorous and definite.

This, the earliest letter of the Apostle Paul which we have, closes with a series of practical injunctions which reach a particular climax in vss. 16-22.

The second letter to the Thessalonians was written shortly afterwards from Corinth. The question of its authenticity and of its relationship to the first letter has admittedly caused scholars many a headache. This is not the place to go into these matters in more detail. The best explanation is that it is genuine and follows closely upon the first letter. The circumstances prevailing in the church are still somewhat the same as those at the time of I Thessalonians. Paul has, however, received some new information (III.11) which impels him to clarify certain points. In spite of his warnings in I Thess. V.1ff., or because they had been misunderstood, many fantastic conceptions of the return of Christ had arisen in Thessalonica; these Paul resisted. This is probably the main reason for the letter.

CH. I pays a fine tribute to the church; it has held fast amidst persecution and affliction. They may on that account wait confidently for Christ's return. But this return of Christ has still to come: the "day of Christ" has not yet dawned. That is the principal theme of CH. II. Paul's own statements may have given rise to such misunderstandings (II.2). The church must therefore realise that Christ will not come before the Antichrist, the "adversary," the "man of sin" has appeared. How are we to explain this assertion?

We must bear in mind that, as a former scribe, Paul was brought up to hold rigid ideas regarding the end of the world. We call these ideas "apocalyptic" from the Greek, and the study of them, together with their literary formulation "Apocalyptic." One conception which belonged to late Jewish apocalyptic was that of the Anti-Messiah, out of which developed the Antichrist of Christianity. Paul was perhaps thinking of the Emperor Caligula who desired to have his portrait set up in the Temple as an object of adoration. Nero was later identified with the Antichrist. The conception of the Antichrist, or rather the Anti-Messiah, reaches back far beyond the Jewish era into primitive religio-historical realms. Many old myths give an account of a conflict at the beginning of time which will be renewed at the end of time. Germanic saga tells of the Midgard-serpent, the arch-enemy of the gods of light. Traces of this myth are to be found in the Old Testament also (cf. Amos ix.3, Isaiah xxx.7, Ps. civ.26, Job iii.8). Provisionally, however, this anti-theistic power is still fettered, a fact of which Paul also speaks (ii.7). Something exists to restrain the mystery of iniquity. Even the earliest expositors assumed that Paul was thinking here of the Roman state and its judicial administration. That is possible, though not certain, but in any event we are dealing here with a pre-Pauline apocalyptic tradition. It is characteristic of the world of apocalyptic thought that although it alludes to historical facts it leaves everything mysteriously vague. We shall have to forego therefore any hope of a completely certain interpretation. The Thessalonians were obviously "in the picture" and knew what Paul meant. We, however, must be content with mere conjecture on this point.

Many readers will be disconcerted at the strangeness of these ideas. But we must not forget two things. First, in many ways even Paul is very much a child of his time, and bound therefore to favour traditional ideas. Secondly, however, he is by means of them pursuing a practical end with which we can only concur and which he reveals in iii.10f. The hope of Christ's return must not lead to mindless fanaticism. The reference to the coming of Antichrist is intended to bolt the door against any kind of fantastic excess. That is the sound and sober intention of the apocalyptic teaching in ch. ii. The exhortations scattered here and there, and the signature written in his own hand at the bottom of the letter (iii.17), both serve this purpose. We owe it to this letter that the Church of Jesus Christ was guarded from the fate which befell many fanatical sects.

# GALATIANS

GALATIANS is also, in the best sense of the word, an "occasional" letter, though it is of far greater basic importance than the two letters to the Thessalonians. For in it Paul saw himself compelled to speak on a fundamental question of his Gospel: the problem of Law and Freedom. How did this come about?

In order to answer this, we must first offer some clarification of a prior question: who are the Galatians to whom Paul is writing? In the history of scholarship two theories stand opposed, designated as the "South Galatian" and "North Galatian" respectively. Both have their powerful protagonists even today. According to the South Galatian theory, by the Galatians are meant the inhabitants of the province of Galatia to which, amongst others, the churches at Iconium, Lystra and Derbe belonged. Several factors are adduced in support of this theory, but one especially: these churches are, according to the account in Acts (Acts XIII and XIV, XVI. Iff.), well known both to the Apostle and to ourselves. On the other hand, we know very little about the Galatians as they are understood by the North Galatian theory, meaning the Celts who had settled in the region of Galatia on the banks of the Halys. Nevertheless this theory deserves preference to the other. The main evidence in support of it lies in the apostrophe "O . . . Galatians" (Gal. III.1). This cannot refer to the inhabitants of the province, who belonged to the most varied races, and amongst whom the actual Galatians clearly stood out by reason of their national and racial individuality. This apostrophe would be almost as much out of place as if someone were to address the Germans in Brazil as "O Brazilians." The fact that Acts tells us almost nothing of the churches in Galatia proper is due to the gaps that we have elsewhere observed in its account. For the rest we do hear that Paul had sojourned in this area during the second missionary journey (Acts XVI.6; cf. Gal. IV.13ff.) Acts XVIII.23 recounts a second visit of the Apostle to this region and in a manner which already presupposes the existence of churches. Paul had thus probably evangelised there on the

first occasion, even though there is no mention of such evange-
lism in Acts xvi.6. We may here omit any other piece of
evidence and shall decide, for the reason stated, in favour of
the North Galatian theory.

What is the occasion of this letter? Galatians is part of Paul's
great struggle with the question of the Law. At the Apostolic
Council in Jerusalem it had been decided not to demand from
Gentile Christians the assumption of the Jewish Law. Paul
had there gained the victory over the extremist Jewish Christians, the so-called Judaisers, and had even convinced the first
apostles of the correctness of his views. In this way he had
scotched the attempts of the Judaisers to exert their influence
in Syrian Antioch, the centre of Gentile Christianity. Nevertheless the Judaisers felt themselves called to continue the work of
undermining the Pauline mission. They therefore attempted to
induce the Galatians to abandon their Pauline freedom. We
can imagine the Galatians to have been people of fickle temperament; and, we may assume, they were not any too firmly
established in the views in which Paul had instructed them.
This explains why they had yielded, as they obviously had, to
the insinuations of the Judaisers. Paul had warned the Galatians about them on his second visit (Gal. iv.13, 1.9). But hardly
had he left them when they were subjected to the renewed influence of the Judaisers (1.6). The latter concentrated their
attack on two points. They sought to undermine the standing
of the Apostle. He did not belong to the Twelve and therefore
lacked true apostolic authority. He had not been called by
Jesus Himself and was entirely dependent upon the original
apostles. He strove for the favour of men (1.10ff.), and was not
consistent; sometimes he rejected the whole Law, sometimes he
would himself teach circumcision (v.11; cf. Acts xvi.3). Besides
these personal attacks, there were those directed against Paul's
teachings. His preaching of the Gospel was only half the truth.
Belief in the Gospel found its fulfilment in obedience to the
Law; only the two together resulted in true Christianity. One
could not be a real Christian without circumcision (v.2ff.)
All this made no small impression upon the intimidated
Galatians. They were already well on the way to yielding to
these demands, and seem already to have adopted the Jewish
calendar of feasts (iv.10).

Paul was in Ephesus when this painful news reached him. He would have preferred to set off immediately in order to put matters right in person (IV.20), but that was not possible, hence his recourse to the pen. The letter is of an explicitly polemical character, and in severity leaves nothing to be desired. It is the only letter of Paul which contains no expression of thanksgiving for the church. With grim sarcasm he advises the zealous champions of circumcision to castrate themselves (V.12). He ruthlessly emphasises the uniqueness of his Gospel, which is second to none (I.6ff.) but his boundless love for the church also finds moving expression (IV.12-20, VI.16). By reason of its personal character and its subject-matter Galatians is one of the most significant utterances of the Apostle. It is so great fundamentally that it ranks as second only to Romans, together with which it exerted a decisive influence upon the Gospel of the Reformation.

The theme of the letter may be summed up as "The Freedom of the Christian Man." Its arrangement is simple and clear:

(1) Defence against personal accusations and the disputing of Paul's apostolic ministry (I and II);
(2) The freedom "from" (III and IV);
(3) The freedom "to" (V and VI).

The first part, which serves as a defence, contains an historical retrospect. It is a valuable source for the life of the Apostle, and as we have already drawn upon it here and there in our historical account, we need not repeat it here. For the rest, we must admire the clear and well-constructed sequence of thought. The self-defence occurs in the form of a gradual crescendo:

(1) Paul was called by Jesus just as directly as the twelve original apostles, and has no need, therefore, to be taught by them (I.11-24).
(2) The first Apostles have had to recognise Paul's work, and, at the Apostolic Council in Jerusalem, sanctioned the unlegalistic Gospel despite the intrigues of the Judaisers (II.1-10).
(3) Paul had actually called Peter to account before the assembled church in Antioch because of his deviation from the unlegalistic Gospel (II.11-21).

After this personal defence Paul turns to the question of the Law's significance. Christ liberates from the Law. The freedom "from" is accordingly the theme of the second part (CHS. III and IV). Paul places two things in sharp antithesis: the preaching of faith and legal piety ("the works of the law," III.1-5). To the preaching of the unlegalistic Gospel the Galatians owe that great internal revolution which they are manifestly experiencing as the reality of the divine Spirit. How can they be so foolish as to wish to complete this visible work of the Holy Spirit by legalistic means ("flesh," III.3)? The Judaisers have probably been telling them something about the Chosen People, and about the sonship of Abraham, available only to the circumcised. For Paul, however, Abraham is the model not of legal piety but of faith. The sonship of Abraham is tied neither to the Law nor to descent, but solely to faith (III.6-9). The Law places men under a curse, since no one can fulfil it completely. But Christ has set us free from this curse, in that He has taken it upon Himself (III.10-14). The divine promise of blessing, made to Abraham on account of his faith and to all believers after him, cannot be annulled by the Law which came much later (III.15-18). Nevertheless the Law still has its significance for the "history of salvation." It can never replace the promise, and therefore the grace of God. But, in so far as it quickens conscience and convinces man of his insufficiency, it has performed a task of preparation for grace and for Christ. This time of preparation is now past. The new "righteousness" lies purely and simply in the fact that we can accept God's gift without any "ifs" or "buts." That is what Paul understands by "faith." The grace of God which faith accepts as a gift turns anxious "men of law" into free children of God. No one is excluded from this sonship of God by his descent or sex or social position (III.19-29). So long, of course, as the son of the house is a minor, he is bound, like any slave, by rules and precepts. But Christ has promoted us to full sonship with all its privileges (IV.1-7). For that reason, the Galatians must not revert to the position of minors. Do they not sense the love which inspires Paul's concern for them? Are they really to let themselves be deluded by the wicked zeal of the Judaisers (IV.8-20)? This part concludes with an allegorical exposition of the Hagar story (IV.21-31). Paul here betrays his rabbinic training. It is difficult for us to understand this kind of allegorical conceit. But, in the conventional form of the day, Paul gives expression to what was, for that time, a highly novel idea. The son of Hagar, the handmaid, typifies for him the Covenant at Sinai, in the centre of which stands the Law. But the Law brings slavery to external precepts. Isaac, the son of Sarah, on the other hand, the son of the wife and thus of the freewoman, was born contrary to all human expectation solely by reason of the divine promise (Gen. XVIII.10f.) He therefore typifies for Paul the Christian who must obtain the glorious liberty of the children of God not by human effort, but only by God's grace.

The man who takes exception to the Jewish terms in which these ideas are clothed should consider what an unheard-of revolutionary effect these ideas must have had upon Jewish sensibilities. Israel, with its pride in the Sinai Covenant, here sees itself reduced to the level of the illegitimate son, while, to the Galatians, whom they contemptuously despised, is granted the sonship of God, which was promised to the posterity of Israel. What an inner revolution it must have meant for Paul before such a point of view became possible to him, the former Pharisee! In face of this passage, how superficial it is to accuse the Apostle of "Jewish thinking"!

The third part (v and vi) deals with the freedom "to." The Christian is free from the Law, but, for that very reason, free to love. Freedom is not licence, which does and allows what it pleases. True freedom knows itself to be summoned to the service of love. Faith is not a "laying-of-hands-in-the-lap," faith is always "working through love" (v.6). This commandment to love is, of course, not rigid outward compulsion, as was characteristic of legal piety, but a free impulse from within. This is what Paul understands by "walking by the Spirit." Love is therefore the fulfilment of the Law (v.14; cf. Rom. XIII.10), and revolutionises the Law from within. The Law says "you must"; the Gospel says "you may." The Law demands performance and promises reward, and yet can provide neither. The Gospel bestows sonship and awakens love, and in this way achieves what is to the Law an impossibility. So the Gospel is at once the fulfilment and the end of the Law. For we cannot travel along both paths at the same time. If we seek any kind of guarantee in our own achievement, we are refusing the gift

of sonship and placing ourselves in the position of slaves. It is
for this reason that Paul so passionately contests the requirement
of circumcision (v.8-21). But no one would wish to maintain
that a true son obliges his father less than a hired slave. The
freedom "from" is therefore the freedom "to." Nevertheless,
the position of son rests not upon the son's achievement, but
simply upon the fact that his father acknowledges him as son.
His position depends upon his birth (vi.15).

We cannot help being gripped by the sublimity and freedom
of these ideas, provided we do not deliberately shut our eyes to
them. There is no disputing the source of Paul's ideas: he
learnt them from Jesus. The Pauline doctrine of Justification is
none other than Jesus's preaching of the sonship of God. Although the form may be different, the meaning is the same. It
was when this message disclosed itself to Luther that the
"freedom of a Christian man" became a reality to him. He
understood it so well because he found himself in a very similar
situation to Paul. He also came from a piety which stood under
the sign of law. Medieval Catholicism resembled late Judaism
in this respect. Seemingly for the modern Protestant the matter
lies otherwise. In general, he knows nothing of the exigencies
of legal piety and thus has no sense of the freedom which the
Gospel in this instance brings. But that is only apparently the
case. Even modern man lives to a great extent in the grip of
a righteousness of works. It makes no fundamental difference
whether it has to do with dogmatic obstinacy, with moral self-
righteousness or with any other kind of self-sufficient attitude.
The result in all cases is "slavery," a state of thraldom. The
letter to the Galatians confronts us also with the question: shall
our relationship to God be determined by performance and
reward, or by trust and the acceptance of a free gift as between
a child and his father? Thank God *we* do not have to answer
this question. God Himself has answered it once and for all in
Jesus Christ. We have nothing to do but to allow the answer
to be spoken to us. Then we shall experience the truth of it as
blessed freedom.

# I CORINTHIANS

THE church in Corinth was a special object of concern to the Apostle. We have already heard about its foundation during the second missionary journey. We also know the social, moral and religious situation which prevailed in this city of world commerce. Paul had left Corinth after two and a half years' activity there. In view of the fact that the two letters to Corinth sketch no very favourable picture of that city's church, it is only too conceivable that the eyes of the Apostle, who had meanwhile secured a new centre of activity in Ephesus, should frequently and anxiously have looked across the sea towards the city on the Isthmus. He wanted to keep in touch with the church by letter at least. A first letter, written before our I Corinthians, has been lost (I Cor. v.9ff.) In it Paul had forbidden any association with fornicators within the church. Our I Corinthians is the answer to various enquiries contained in a letter from the church (I Cor. VII.1). Various facts concerning the church's life had come to Paul's ears by other routes also (I.11, V.1, XI.18). Traffic between the two maritime cities of Corinth and Ephesus was lively, so that Paul would have been kept up-to-date with circumstances in the Greek metropolis. I Corinthians is even more of an occasional letter than Galatians. As Paul deals with the enquiries of the Corinthians point by point the letter lacks any clear sequence of thought. But the inner thread connecting the answers and advice of the Apostle stands out all the more clearly. It is this inner thread which gives this letter lasting significance even though the circumstances with which it deals have meanwhile completely altered. Here again the truly apostolic art of setting purely temporary situations in the light of an ultimate perspective inspires our admiration.

The first section of the letter is directed against party spirit in the Corinthian church. Some swear by the person of Paul, others by that of Apollos; a third group calls itself after Peter (Aramaic: Cephas); a fourth describes itself proudly as the Christ party (I.12). Apollos is known to us from Acts (XVIII.24ff.)

He appears to have been a brilliant speaker, full of profound thought, a true Alexandrine. We can easily imagine the impression he made upon the Greek mentality of the Corinthians (Acts XIX.1). In this respect he was evidently superior to Paul. He was not responsible for the formation of parties; at the time I Corinthians was written he was on the best of terms with Paul in Ephesus (I Cor. XVI.12). The Cephas and Christ parties appear to have borne a more Jewish Christian stamp. Charges were being made against Paul from this direction similar to those we have found in the case of the Judaisers in Galatians (I Cor. IX.1ff., XVI.8f.) This applies particularly to members of the Christ party, as we may deduce from hints in II Corinthians (II Cor. XI.22f., v.16, XI.18). Paul attacks this party spirit in the first four chapters (1.10-IV.21). Where Christ is Lord the cult of personality is impossible (1.13). The Apollos party are proud of their wisdom and understanding (*gnosis*), over against which Paul sets the "folly of the Cross." But this "folly" and this "stumbling-block" comprise the most profound and hidden wisdom of God. In the light of Christ's Cross Paul experiences a transvaluation of all values. In his "theology of the Cross" Paul develops thoughts of an unfathomable profundity. In this respect Luther later became Paul's faithful pupil, when he set the Christian Gospel as a "theology of the Cross" in opposition to every kind of "theology of honour." God's act in Christ compels even our thinking to repent, to "turn round." Greek intellectualism finds itself in the same situation *vis-à-vis* the revelation in Christ as Jewish moralism does. Both prove themselves incapable, as against the Cross, of being a direct road for man to God. Human wisdom could not itself imagine the nature of God as revealed in the Cross of Christ. Where human wisdom does not acknowledge this it becomes folly in the eyes of God (1.18-25). It is worth while to ponder upon these thoughts, for they give Paul a place, though an unsought one, in the ranks of mankind's deepest thinkers. The repercussions of his views can easily be detected even amongst the greatest minds in German history. Genuine thought can in no way ignore the reality of the Cross if it is to be preserved from illusion. How superficial many a "philosophy" appears in contrast to this "theology of the Cross"! Paul finds the truth of it confirmed in the composition of the

church (1.26-31), and in the manner of his own arrival in Corinth (II.1-5). This also is "wisdom," certainly not earthly but
divine, perceived only by the man in whom God's Spirit is at
work (II.6-16). Party spirit, however, is a sign of materialism
(III.1-4). Human work needs no glorification, for it will receive
its judgment from God (III.5-15). The Church of God belongs
to no religious leader, but to Christ, and thus to God (III.16-23).
The apostles, however, are servants of Christ, no more and no
less, and in fact they share, to a certain degree, the humiliation
of Christ. There is thus no place for boasting here (IV.1-13).
Paul wishes to spare the Corinthians shame when he comes;
for this reason they must pay heed to him beforehand and get
rid of the partisan attitude (IV.14-21).

In CH. V Paul takes up a particularly serious case. A member
of the church is living in an immoral relationship with his step-
mother. The Apostle knows only one method of dealing with
this: the incestuous man must be ruthlessly expelled from the
church (V.1-5). Fornication such as marked the orgies in
Corinth was intolerable within the church. A man cannot
belong both to Christ and to a harlot (V.6-13, VI.9-20). Nor
should Christians bring their domestic disputes before heathen
judges. If a dispute is unavoidable it should at least be settled
within the church (VI.1-8).

Sexual questions evidently played no small part in the church
at Corinth. Some, still under the spell of their heathen past,
were for giving full play to their desires, and arrogantly gave as
their reasons their "Christian liberty" and their "knowledge."
Another group tended towards complete sexual asceticism.
Paul turns to them in CH. VII. He, for his own part, feels as they
do. However, as ability to abstain is a gift that is bestowed upon
only a few he has no intention of forbidding marriage (VII.1-9).
Existing marriages need not be dissolved, even if one spouse is
still pagan. On the whole, everyone should remain where he
has been placed (VII.10-24). Even if a slave could become free
he should rather remain a slave (VII.21: R.V. mg.) In the following passage Paul betrays the motive for his own aversion to
marriage: it is no longer expedient to tie oneself to the world
in this way, for the end is at hand. The single person is, in the
Apostle's view, freer to serve the Lord than the married person
(VII.25-40). There is hardly a chapter in Paul's letters that

leaves us so dissatisfied as this one, for it betrays a real limitation of the great Apostle. He sees only the sexual aspect of marriage and does not see that it is also a spiritual and moral partnership. That is a flaw which cannot be ignored. But was it very different in the world of Socrates? We must not impose our standards upon past ages without compromise. The Church has not canonised the assertions made here in spite of its high and centuries-old regard for asceticism. Besides 1 Cor. VII the New Testament contains the so-called "house-tables" (Eph. v.22-vi.9, Col. III.18-iv.1), which sketch an essentially different picture of the family relationship. Whether they derive from Paul is uncertain. The point is that Christian morality did exercise an ennobling influence upon the family life of antiquity.

A further question that worried the Corinthians was whether it was permissible to eat meat sacrificed to idols (VIII-x). We must distinguish two things here: the eating of this meat in itself and participation in meals where sacrifices are made to idols. Only a portion of the sacrificial animal was burnt upon the altar. The greater part came upon the meat market or was consumed at cult meals in private homes. Christians can eat any meat that comes upon the market without having any scruples (x.23-33). But if a Christian brother takes exception to this one should forego it rather than wound the other's conscience. Voluntary renunciation of that to which one is entitled can, under certain circumstances, be a Christian duty. The Apostle demonstrates this by his own example (IX). In order not to give offence he has renounced all financial support on the part of the Church, although he could demand it as a right. The Christian life is a serious matter which demands complete dedication (IX.24-27). Life is hazardous, so "let any one who thinks that he stands take heed lest he fall" (x.1-13). Paul advocates that Christians should be left free to decide for themselves about the sacrifice of meat to idols. But this liberty extends only as far as it can be indulged without one's own conscience, or that of the "weak" brother, having misgivings. To act contrary to one's conscience is, in any case, harmful. The position is different where participation in avowedly-ritual sacrificial meals in a pagan temple or cult fellowship is concerned. This is forbidden to Christians. To participate in them is to enter into communion with the idols, whose demonic nature Paul does not wholly deny. One cannot share in Christ's supper and at the same time practise table fellowship with demons. For in neither case are we dealing with external forces of no consequence but with a reality, divine or demonic in character, into which we are incorporated through participation in the meal (VIII.1-13, X.14-29).

CHS. XI-XIV form a fresh unity in which Paul directs himself against abuses in the conduct of worship. Certain women in the Corinthian church have misinterpreted their Christian freedom and exempted themselves from the ancient rule about wearing the veil in public gatherings. Paul condemns them severely. The Gospel has nothing to do with revolution and emancipation as such; its aim is not to change the world's outward appearance, but rather its inner character. He has no intention, therefore, of disturbing traditional customs as long as they are not actually anti-religious (XI.1-16). Worse still are the abuses connected with the celebration of Holy Communion, or, as it is called here, the "Lord's supper" (XI.17-34). At that time the celebration took place in quite different conditions from nowadays. The church came together for a proper communal meal, the so-called "love feast" (agape). This custom doubtless had associations with the institution, common on Graeco-Roman soil, of cult meals celebrated by religious fraternities, the expenses of which were defrayed by the communal funds or by the contributions of individuals. The celebration of the Lord's Supper proper was the climax of this love feast, the whole thing expressing in a wonderful fashion the primitive Church's life of faith and love: Communion with the Lord and communion of the brethren with one another. The Apostle is affected all the more painfully, therefore, by the abuses reported to him. The rich are turning the love feast into a revel. Instead of unselfishly sharing what they have brought with the poorer members, they think only of their own satisfaction. In this way they profane the Sacrament. How can they so shamefully transgress the commandment to love, when the Lord Himself is present amongst them at His meal? If they do not distinguish the "body of the Lord" from ordinary eating and drinking, then the presence of Christ becomes a judgment upon them. Indeed, there has already been judgment. It operates even in the physical sphere; many are sick, some have died (XI.30). Because of this passage Paul has been accused of holding a "magical" conception of the Sacrament, but this accusation is unjustified. The Body and Blood of Christ are not, in Paul's view, charms. They are certainly representative, however, of the full reality and presence of Christ in the Sacrament. This presence can signify grace or judgment, and that upon the whole man, body and soul. Paul has no use for that spurious mysticism in which all reality evaporates into the realm of the so-called "spiritual." Herein lies his sacramental realism, which has no connexion, however, with superstitious beliefs.

Church gatherings in Corinth must have presented a lively and colourful picture. Things did not proceed in them with the formality and the stiff solemnity which mark our own. The wind of the Spirit could be seen there, roaring through these young churches like a spring storm, and sometimes causing exceedingly strange occurrences. One of the most remarkable "spiritual gifts" was that of speaking with tongues. This phenomenon probably first arose at Pentecost. At least, the narrative in Acts II (cf. especially Acts II.13) only becomes really comprehensible when read in the light of I Cor. XII-XIV. The phenomenon consisted of an ecstatic and rapturous babbling that remained incomprehensible to its hearers, but in which the ecstatic felt himself to be completely dominated by a higher power. Such phenomena are generally alien to us sober and critical Europeans, but they often occurred in the religions of the Near East. They even gained entrance into Hellenism in the form of the "dionysiac." The Corinthians at any rate prided themselves upon this gift particularly—indeed, those endowed with it despised those furnished with different spiritual gifts (XII.7-10), a fact which immediately made possession of this gift fatal. Paul does not doubt its reality: he himself possesses it to the fullest possible degree (XIV.18). What he does reject outright, however, is the arrogance which the Corinthians combine with it. For him, the relative importance of the various gifts of the spirit depends upon their value for the community as a whole. The Church is *one* body, in which every member has its task, and in which none can do without, or look down upon, the other (XII.4-31). If one wishes, however, to evaluate individual gifts, then the most excellent is that which serves the cause of love.

In this context, Paul sings the "Canticle of Love" (1 Cor. xiii), and by virtue of this, apart from anything else, his letters rank among the most wonderful things written in human language. Paul has rightly been called the "apostle of faith." But even John, "the apostle of love," never spoke more profoundly and more warmly of love than Paul. Love, for Paul, is the touchstone of all that is true (xiii.1-3). It is in its meekness the greatest power on earth (xiii.4-7), indeed it binds heaven and earth together (xiii.8-13). It is the only thing that God and man have completely in common; in it, therefore, time and eternity are one. It alone is of eternal duration. This love must not be confused, of course, with that other common emotion which men also call love. Human love generally contains an element of self-love, even where, as in the Platonic *eros*, it is the spiritualised form of love for the ideal and the idea. Even this love serves the cause of self-enrichment. Christian love resembles divine love in that it "does not insist upon its own way" (xiii.5). In this incomparably simple statement Paul expresses its deepest essence. But, we may ask, is any such thing to be found on earth? Has not Paul overreached himself here? To that there is only one answer: the Apostle can speak thus because this love became man in Jesus Christ. Since then earth's deepest meaning has been a heavenly one.

> I have come to know man in his profoundest essence,
> I know the world down to its innermost core.
> I know that love, and again love, is its veriest soul,
> And that my mission in life is to love evermore.
> (Morgenstern)

Certainly, on earth everything is still fragmentary (xiii.9-12); but in love the outlines of divine perfection are already taking shape.

It is in this divine perspective that Paul once again sets the question of the significance of "tongues" for the life of the Church (xiv). Speaking with tongues is good, but prophetic preaching ("prophesying") is better. For the one serves only for personal edification, but the other for that of the Church and the winning of non-believers; let the ecstatic utterance find expression in intelligible language ("with the mind," xiv.1-25). The spirit must certainly not be quenched (xiv.39; cf. 1 Thess. v.19). But everything should serve to edify (xiv.26), and be done in a decent and orderly manner (xiv.40). Thus, with loving hand, Paul smoothes the chaotic surging of the Spirit in this strangely excited church, and is able at the same time to unravel and straighten the entangled threads of historically-conditioned religious phenomena in the light of a Christianity which is timeless and universal.

The question of the resurrection of the dead seems to have specially worried the Corinthians. This explains the sudden transition to this theme in ch. xv. Paul's preaching of the Resurrection had already met with no approval in Athens. It had now caused difficulties to the Corinthians also. It is unlikely that they materialistically denied the possibility of life after death—on the contrary, there were many in Greece at that time who dreamed of the immortality of the soul. Paul, however, stands not for the immortality of the soul, but for the resurrection of the whole man. The conception of the resurrection of the body derives from late Judaism, but it is more in accordance with the final Christian hope than is immortality of the soul only. The biblical hope goes beyond a mere "spiritualism." It knows of a promise for the whole of creation, even for the corporeal world. The corporeal world itself comes from God, and therefore has a relationship to eternity. In this respect the Christian doctrine takes the material world far more seriously than does the platonic idealism of Greece, of which the repercussions are still affecting us today. That is the realism of the biblical world-view which Paul himself wholeheartedly professes.

Paul begins with the fact of Easter, proved by the appearances of the Risen Lord, of which the experience near Damascus is one (xv.1-11). For Paul, however, the resurrection of Christians is the certain consequence of the Resurrection of Christ (xv.12-22). If there is no resurrection of the dead, then Christ was not raised (vs. 13). How does Paul come to make this, at first glance, astonishing statement? It is explained by his conception of "being-in-Christ" (see p. 44). On Easter Day God's new world invaded this order of reality. The man who belongs to Christ has thereby been translated, in a sense, into the divine world; this process will be completed at the resurrection of the dead. By reason of his physical birth the Christian belongs to the world of Adam, that is, to the world of transience and of death;

in spirit, however, he belongs to the world of Christ, that is God's world, the world of the resurrection and the life (xv.20-22). He has indeed become "one body" with Christ (x.16, vi.19, iii.16). With his whole existence therefore, he shares the fate of Christ's body (cf. Rom. vi.8f.) It follows that the man who wishes to deny the possibility of resurrection for himself must also deny it for Christ. But this would mean that our faith would descend to the level of illusion (xv.14-19). For if God's world has not, in Christ, triumphed over this transient world, then we still remain under the curse of utter hopelessness. The reality of death and transitoriness would be more powerful than any idealism, however well-intentioned, that attempted to ignore this reality. Victory would then go to the materialistic slogan: "Let us eat and drink, for tomorrow we die" (xv.32). But Christ's Resurrection has become the first act in the great drama of the end of history (xv.23-28). God will reserve the last word for Him; no other reality will ultimately withstand His reality.

One cannot lead a Christian life without faith in the Resurrection. This fact is confirmed as much by the practice in the Corinthian church of having oneself baptised for the unbaptised dead as by the Apostle's attitude to life (xv.29-34). But as far as the form of the resurrected body is concerned we must eschew all crudely material conceptions (xv.35-49). The resurrected body will be different from the earthly. There is doubtless a connexion between the two; but the resurrected body does not grow organically out of the earthly—it arises only by virtue of an act of creation on God's part. We must not be misled here by the image of the seed and the plant. Paul is not stressing what, to our way of thinking, would be the important thing, namely the organic relationship between the two, but rather the dying of the seed and God's free creation of the plant. We must not here transfer our scientific thinking to Paul. The resurrection is simply a divine miracle, no more and no less than was the Resurrection of Christ Himself.

At the end of the chapter Paul once again demonstrates the outlook with which we are already familiar from 1 Thessalonians. Many will still experience the return of Christ and, with it, the beginning of the end. But even their bodies will be transformed, for God's kingdom has absolutely nothing in common with the earthly order of things. Paul concludes his arguments with a song of triumph (xv.50-58). This is followed (xvi) by instructions for the collection destined for the Christians in Jerusalem (Gal. ii.10), personal messages and a greeting written in his own hand.

Many were the cares which caused Paul to write this letter, but think what Christendom has gained from it! Truly, God often uses strange means of realising His saving purposes.

# II CORINTHIANS

THE second letter to the Corinthians falls in the period after Paul's departure from Ephesus. At the time of writing Paul was in Macedonia. The events leading up to the letter, and the external circumstances under which it was written, have already been described above in the chapter on the so-called third missionary journey. We shall not repeat them here.

II Corinthians is the most personal of all Paul's letters. Nowhere do we see so deeply into the Apostle's heart as here, a fact which gives this letter particular importance. We must not, of course, interpret it as an outpouring of the heart. We might call it a reluctant confession, for Paul does not willingly speak about himself. It is his way as an apostle to concentrate entirely on the cause. His letters are not intended to be understood as the "confessions of a beautiful soul," but as confessions of the Lord Jesus Christ. But here, in the second letter, Paul finds himself in the peculiar position of being obliged, for the sake of the cause, to speak personally. For, in the Corinthians' eyes, the authority of the cause which Paul represents depends on the apostolic authority of his person, which he must protect against every form of attack, both furtive and open. So Paul once again finds himself compelled to do something that he would not dream of doing voluntarily. It is fascinating and gripping to observe the conflicting emotions working in the Apostle's soul. This fiery spirit was endowed with a tender heart, and yet he could, where necessary, work himself up to the greatest sternness and severity. Modest reticence was more natural to him, but, when obliged to, he could lay bare the innermost depths of his heart. Because of the personal character of this letter and its many historical allusions, much of it remains obscure. But here, once again, is seen the apostolic genius for lifting the personal and transient into the sphere of the supra-personal and timeless.

The letter falls into three parts: CHS. I-VII, VIII and IX, and X-XIII. The first part is an account and defence of Paul's apostolic ministry and message. The second part turns upon an urgent practical task of the moment, namely the collection for the Jerusalem church. The third part is a defence of the Apostle's personal standing and a caustic settling of accounts with his old opponents, the Judaisers. The unity of this letter has often been disputed. But the various suggestions put forward for dividing it up all encounter serious difficulties. The unevenness of the letter is most easily accounted for by the obvious pauses in dictation. One further thing must be noted when reading II Corinthians: Paul often employs here his opponents' turns of speech. It must be understood, therefore, that a great deal of it is not the Apostle's own opinion and must be placed, as it were, in quotation marks. Paul not infrequently shows himself in the process to be a master of irony, an irony permeated, however, with his sincerity and goodness.

The letter, which has so much to say about suffering, begins with a prayer of thanksgiving to the God of all comfort (1.1-14). If Paul altered his original itinerary, it was not because he was vacillating or failing to take things seriously, but rather because he was concerned for the Corinthians (1.15-24). One proof of his love should be the "tearful letter" (II.1-4). The church member by whom Paul was offended on his interim visit (see p. 92) has been punished sufficiently. Paul has forgiven him and the church should do likewise (II.5-11). His love for the church has given the Apostle no rest in Troas, despite the success of his preaching there; the news which Titus has brought fills him with thanksgiving. Paul here reaches the actual theme of the first part: the defence and praise of his apostolic ministry (III-VII). Paul does not need, like others, to commend himself and to boast. His best recommendation is the church itself and his glory consists not in his own cleverness but in the ministry in which God has placed him (III.1-6). This ministry of the New Covenant has a far greater glory than that of the Old Covenant. In a powerful antithesis Paul compares the Old and New Covenants. Here perhaps he is aiming obliquely at his Judaising opponents who wished to fuse Christ and Moses. The Sinai Covenant was the dispensation of the letter, that is, of external precept, of the Law, that cannot give life, but only convinces man of his helplessness and thereby delivers him up to perdition. For a true understanding we must here recall the arguments in Galatians. In the New Covenant it is not the letter, but the Spirit of God, which holds sway, this being none other than the exalted Lord Christ Himself (III.17). The Spirit of God works not from without as rigid precept but from within as life-giving power (III.6). Where He is active, therefore, freedom reigns. Here Paul once again acknowledges the "freedom of a Christian man." The revelation of the Old Covenant, compared with that of the New, does not deserve to be called "revelation." For believers in the Old Covenant the veil of Moses hangs even today over the Old Testament; only in the light of Christ can it be properly understood. Christians, however, are destined to reflect the radiance of Christ and to be transformed into His likeness (III.7-18). This light of Christ, comparable, in its origin, to the light of the first day of Creation, has shone in the heart of the Apostle (Damascus—IV.6) and effects, therefore, a transformation that has no need to shrink from the light (IV.1-6).

In what is admittedly strange contrast to the glory of this ministry stands the lowliness of the servant. But that must be so, for this service is a following of the Cross. The dying of the outer man serves to renew the inner man: "He must increase, but I must decrease" (Jn. III.30)—that is the law to which the Apostle's service is subject. Paul is here preaching a practical "theology of the Cross." His dying ministers at the same time to the life of the Church; and it is in this way that the law of Christ operates in his apostolic ministry. So God trains His servant to turn his attention towards the things that are invisible. That is apostolic "idealism" (IV.7-18). Eternity is not for Paul the Great Unknown about which we can make no pronouncement. Its content is Christ. He would prefer, of course, to be clothed rather than unclothed; that is, he hopes for a transformation of this his earthly body into a resurrected body (cf. 1 Cor. XV.51), without having to go through the valley of the shadow of death. But the prospect of being at home with his Lord enables him to overcome his fear of death. The thought of the judgment also imparts an eternal direction to his life (V.1-10). He is no longer limited by earthly considerations. Dying and resurrection with Christ acquire validity even for everyday life. Everything is bathed in the light of Easter. If therefore the Judaisers accuse Paul of not having known Jesus, their reproach is quite unfounded (v.16). Our new creation has become a reality through God's act of reconciliation in Christ. The Apostle's prayer is that it might also become for the Corinthians the major reality of their lives (v.11-21).

If only we do not forfeit this grace! That is the chief concern of the Apostle in the conduct of his ministry generally, with its heights and depths, its privation and its promise (vi.1-10). That is also, however, his concern with regard to the Corinthians (vi.11-18). But now joy and gratitude can predominate. The Corinthians have manifested a fruitful regret and Titus has been able to return to Paul with good news (vii.1-16).

After a lengthy pause in dictation Paul turns to the second part of his letter (viii and ix). The good example of the Macedonians will encourage the Corinthians to contribute generously, for their part, to the collection for the mother church in Jerusalem. Christ Himself gave His wealth to supply our poverty (viii.1-11). No one will be asked for more than he can afford (viii.12-15). Such an accusation as that the Apostle is not handling the money honestly must be rejected (viii.16-24). Everything should be ready by the time Paul comes (ix.1-5), so that the Corinthians can experience the blessing of joyful giving (ix.6-15).

The third part of the letter (x-xiii) begins without any clear transition. While Paul has so far struck, for the most part, a conciliatory note, there now follows a sudden change of mood, the psychological reasons for which are unknown to us. Perhaps the Apostle had once more succumbed, during a lengthy pause in dictation, to anxiety on account of the Judaisers who had infiltrated into the church. Perhaps, when he had read through what he had so far written, it had appeared to him that this anxiety had not found adequate expression, and that a sharp and unmistakable word was required. The altered tone of the last four chapters can be explained in this way, without the necessity to detach it from the main body of the letter, making it a separate item. Many passages in the third part must be read in inverted commas, consisting, as they do, of accusations against which Paul had still to defend himself.

The church must not underestimate Paul's ability to fight (x.1-6). In this respect he in no way, either in his letters or in his life, falls short of his opponents, who interfere in what does

not concern them. He would prefer to leave it to them to in-
dulge in vainglory (x.7-18), but as the Corinthians evidently
expect such boasting on the part of their leaders he will commit
this folly for their sakes (xi.1). Three times he does this against
his own inclination (xi.1, xi.16, xii.1). He is not inferior to the
Judaisers, whom he designates ironically as the "superlative
apostles" (xi.5). Even if he is no orator, he does not lack
understanding. His modesty was not just a pose. The whole
manner of his arrival was decided entirely by his love for the
church. He must now all the more ruthlessly strip the Judaisers
of their disguise (xi.1-15). They boast of their earthly privileges? They brag of their descent? They boast of their
services for Christ? Very well then, he need not shrink from
any comparison in this connexion. A shocking catalogue of the
Apostle's sufferings should be sufficient proof to the Corinthians. Of course, to the man who has experienced such things,
boasting is out of the question; he can glory only in his weakness
(xi.16-30). Even then Paul has by no means recounted everything, and in the course of writing another such experience
occurs to him (xi.31-33).

But Paul is still not finished with his "boasting." Perhaps
his opponents have also been parading their visions, although
this need not be assumed. At any rate, Paul can claim to have
experienced such an "abundance of revelations" (xii.7) himself. It is significant that during the whole period of his activity
in Corinth he had not breathed a word about this. Only now,
when the Corinthians and his opponents compel him to boast,
does he come to speak of these, his greatest experiences; but
even here he turns aside immediately and extols the power of
Christ over his weakness (xii.1-10).

What Paul here describes with modest reticence ("I know a
man") is a genuine ecstatic experience. We shall miss its
proper meaning if we only interpret it metaphorically. Paul is
here thinking of literal realities. According to the prevailing
view there were seven heavens; in the third heaven lay Paradise.
During the ecstasy the normal bodily functions were suspended;
the ecstatic found himself in a kind of trance. The revelations
which came to him in the process could not and might not be
expressed in human language. The history of religion yields
numerous examples of such experiences. They have become

foreign to the modern Protestant; but he has no right on that account to deny their reality without qualification or banish them to the realm of the pathological. We must not make our modern outlook absolute or normative for all ages. Who knows whether earlier generations were not superior to us in this respect? At any rate Paul himself is convinced of the reality of his experience, and even the modern reader cannot avoid being impressed by his description of it.

All the more impressive is the transition from this "abundance of revelations" to the confession of his weakness. What exactly is meant by the thorn or stake in the flesh can no longer be firmly established. It must have to do with a chronic malady. It is doubtful whether Gal. iv.14 really refers to an eye-disease (see p. 77). Epilepsy has been considered a possibility, particularly on account of the expression "to harass" (literally "strike with the fists"). That is not out of the question, but cannot be proved with any certainty. It was probably some kind of nervous affliction, which would fit in with the temporary blindness near Damascus. This feature, far from diminishing Paul's stature, only serves to enhance it beyond comprehension. What a lifetime of achievement was wrested from his sick body! He would certainly have said: "It was not I who achieved this, but the power of Christ made perfect in my weakness"! Again, we are confronted with the Apostle's practical theology of the Cross. This man could understand the Cross of Christ so deeply because it had become the greatest reality of his life. The ground of his boasting lies paradoxically, therefore, in the fact that there was no cause for him to boast about anything.

Paul's boasting is at an end. He has "become a fool in glorying" (xii.11: A.V.) Once more he defends his apostolic ministry, confirmed by signs and miracles and by his personal sincerity. It is hard for him not to grow bitter (xii.13). At his third visit a settlement must be reached, if necessary, with all urgency (xii.20-xiii.10). God's truth must indeed triumph. So the letter ends on a threatening note. But once more the Apostle's love for his Corinthians breaks through, and he greets them with the apostolic blessing (xiii.13).

In theological and doctrinal content and in the clarity of its thought ii Corinthians is inferior to Romans and Galatians. But Paul is never greater as a Christian and a man than he is here.

# ROMANS

THE beginnings of Christianity in Rome are veiled in mystery—we do not know by what paths it arrived there. According to Rom. xv.22f. a church must already have been in existence in Rome "for many years." From the reference of the Roman writer Suetonius to the expulsion of the Jews from Rome under the emperor Claudius (cf. Acts xviii.2), we can infer that the Gospel had spread comparatively widely among the Roman Jewish community at that time. This was in the year A.D. 49 or A.D. 50. We do not know who precisely were the missionaries or apostles who came as the first messengers of Christ to Rome. But it is only natural that the Gospel should have gained an early entrance into the city upon which all lines, spiritual, political and economic, converged.

Paul wrote to the Romans in the new year of A.D. 58, towards the end of his final stay of approximately three months in Corinth (see p. 93). Thus these three powerful documents, I Corinthians, II Corinthians and Romans, all arose within the space of a year. The occasion of Romans is to be found in the Apostle's itinerary. Paul intended to evangelise in Spain (Rom. xv.24) once the Gospel had penetrated into the main centres of the eastern half of the Empire (xv.23). Others had already laboured in Rome before him. Paul, here again taking scrupulous care not to encroach on another's territory, was aiming for Spain by way of Italy. But, for this mission on the western boundary of the ancient world, he wished to be certain of a base in Rome (xv.24). Quite apart from this, it was self-evident that he could not heedlessly by-pass the church in the capital of the world, on his way to Spain. The letter to the Romans was to prepare for this visit, which Paul had often intended to make (xv.22). In it Paul introduces himself to the church in Rome, and the letter is intended to give them an accurate picture of his conception of the Gospel. In the process, reference to concrete situations recedes entirely into the background. Only CHS. xiv and xv, demanding consideration for the "weak," deal more specifically with such situations. On the other hand, we cannot speak, as some do, of a conflict brewing between Jewish Christians and Gentile Christians in the Roman church. CHS. I-III and IX-XI, which have given rise to this assumption, contrast, not Gentile Christianity and Jewish Christianity, but Gentile, or Gentile Christian, and Jew. The debating opponent whom Paul set up for himself in Romans is not the Judaiser but the Jew. Unlike Galatians, Romans is not a polemical writing but a positive exposition of the Pauline Gospel. The main storms lay behind him when Paul applied himself in Corinth to this most powerful and thoughtful of his letters. In it he presents a final "balance sheet" of his work. The dispute with Judaism clearly occupied the foreground, for it was for him, the former Pharisee, the great problem of his life. Thus even this most "theological" letter reflects the Apostle's personal experience. The first three chapters can be understood precisely as his own interpretation of the Damascus experience. Romans is thus the Apostle's most powerful theological confession.

Its character as an essentially positive exposition of the Pauline views is demonstrated in the clear thought-structure of the letter. Its theme is the "righteousness of God," expounded in four stages:

(1) How is it offered and appropriated? (I-IV);

(2) What does it signify for the Christian? (V-VIII);

(3) How is it demonstrated in the fate of Israel? (IX-XI);

(4) What practical results does it have for the life of the Christian? (XII-XV).

After a full preliminary salutation (1.1-7) and some words of gratitude and affection (1.8-15), Paul quickly takes up his theme (1.16f.) In the Gospel God's righteousness is offered to those who have faith. These words sum up the articles of the Pauline doctrine of Justification. For a general understanding of them the reader is referred once more to what was said at the end of the chapter on Damascus (see pp. 43f.)

After this subject-heading the question in the first part is put in its negative form (1.18-III.20). Men have not attained righteousness on their road to God, but must rather fear his punitive justice. For Paul mankind is divided into two groups: Gentiles and Jews. In their advance towards God both have fallen short of their goal and have therefore failed to attain righteousness. The Gentiles possess a natural perception of God; God has declared Himself to them in nature (1.18ff.) and in their conscience (II.14f.) As in the Areopagus speech Paul does not here deny them a natural religion. Man is therefore, according to Paul, a religious being. God has created him, as distinct from other creatures, in His own image (Gen. 1.27). Man is by nature endowed with the longing for God. But he has abused natural religion. He has turned man's connexion with God into God's connexion with man. That is the sin of the Gentiles. They have debased God's divinity to a human level, and have exchanged God for idols (1.18-23). God's judgment upon this perversion of religion into something that is its very negation has not been wanting. Paul sees it already at work in the terrible spectacle of the decadence of the ancient world.

Nothing would be more futile, however, than, in face of this religious and moral decadence, to set oneself up as a censorious moraliser. The preaching of repentance always, in the first instance, demands one's own repentance. All men run the risk of playing the moraliser. But it was a particular danger where the Judaism of that time was concerned. For this reason Paul turns, in CH. II, to the Jew, who for Paul, himself an offspring of Judaism, was the typical representative of this moralising attitude. The Jew of those days regarded himself as thoroughly superior to the Gentile. But let him beware of finding himself the victim of an illusion (II.1-16)! The sin of the moral, "decent" man appears more refined and is cloaked by a morality which eschews the crudest sins, but it is no less sin in God's eyes. On the contrary, because of its loveless censoriousness this "refined" sin weighs more heavily in the balance than the "crude" sin of the pleasure-seekers. God does not concern Himself with what a man is in the eyes of his fellows (II.11), with whether he is a "Jew" or a "Gentile," a moralist or a libertine. God's judgment is directed according to a man's deeds (II.6). This is a surprising pronouncement for Paul to make, for does not Paul teach, as his central tenet, righteousness by grace alone, through faith (III.28)? How can judgment according to works be reconciled with it (cf. also II Cor. v.10)? Underlying this surprise, however, there is a one-sided conception of Paulinism, such as is widespread in relation to Luther's teaching. Certainly our salvation is based not upon our achievement, but solely upon God's free gift apprehended in faith. Thus the expression "by faith alone" is valid; but faith is never "alone." There is no faith that is not continually expressed in "works." Faith is not a matter of the head or the intellect, but of the whole man, and thus it goes without saying that "doing" is a part of true faith. Faith is not idleness but a "living, energetic, active thing" (Luther). For Paul, therefore, justification by grace alone through faith, and judgment according to works form, not a contradiction, but a unity. The Gentiles also are aware of God's demands upon us—their conscience is for them what the Law is for Israel (II.12-16).

Paul once more warns the Jew, who possesses the Law, against arrogance (II.17-29). He may have the Law and the "sacrament" of circumcision. But neither is of use, indeed they condemn him all the more, if he does not see their practical consequences. The stern indictment of Jewish morality that Paul makes here has its precedent in the Lord Jesus's censure of Pharisaism—both were intended to show the worthlessness of superficial morality as opposed to behaviour really guided by conscience. Paul's proposition must have been a provocation to the Jews. Paul senses this and therefore raises various objections to his argument (III.1-8). Certainly Law and circumcision are not to be depised. God's faithfulness (III.3; A.V. "faith") is not annulled by our unfaithfulness. Even our sin serves to glorify God, but it is no less sin on that account (III.5-8).

That, therefore, is the judgment that Paul pronounces upon man's striving after God. Here Jews and Gentiles are in essentially the same position. They have not attained righteousness before God and are therefore subject to His righteousness. Paul's twofold division of humanity into Jews and Gentiles is applicable only to his time. But, at the same time, they both represent a type that appears everywhere in every age. The "Gentile" stands for all adherents of "natural religion," who seek a path to God apart from attachment to the Church and revelation. The condemnation of the "Jew" demonstrates the dangers of every ecclesiastical attitude. Any form of ecclesiastical piety, or indeed of Bible Christianity, that is self-sufficient and fails to see itself as subject to divine scrutiny, becomes a legalism forfeiting grace. Such a Christ-

ianity is no better than any other human religion, and stands
level with them under God's judgment.

So far Paul has given a negative answer to the question in the
first section. Neither natural religion nor legal piety has reached
its goal. Man's striving after God has not led to God. But
here is the great miracle of God's grace: God Himself has set
out upon the road and has come to meet man in Jesus Christ,
just as the father in the parable goes to meet and embrace his
lost son. That is the great "but now" of the Gospel which
animates Paul's message, and which Paul himself experienced
near Damascus (III.21-31). It was then, when he was treading
the road to God in his own righteousness, that he broke down;
but God intercepted him upon the road in the person of Jesus
Christ. The Apostle has known ever since that there is only
one true way to God, namely God's way to man—and that
way is Jesus Christ. To grant that God is right in this makes a
man righteous, that is, righteous in God's eyes. This "granting
that God is right" Paul calls "faith." Faith is the unqualified
and unconditional acceptance of the divine gift without "ifs"
or "buts." Faith is the renunciation of the "works of the law"
as a means of meriting God's grace. For this grace is present in
Jesus Christ and needs only to be grasped. In Jesus Christ
God's forgiveness is made real and visible. God has put Him
forward as a means of expiation (III.25). Luther translates it
*Gnadenstuhl* ("mercy-seat"), and is here thinking of the lid of
the Ark of the Covenant upon which, annually, at the Feast of
the Atonement, the High Priest sprinkled the blood of the
sacrificial animal. This interpretation is possible. Accordingly,
belief in forgiveness is not merely a human dream, too good to
be true, or just a case of wishful thinking—in Jesus Christ this
truth has indeed become reality. This, of course, has the effect
of exposing all human arrogance as illusion (III.27). Religion
has been freed from perversion and set to rights. Everything
now depends upon God's action—for Jew and Gentile alike
(III.29f.) That is the message of Justification by grace alone
through faith, for Christ's sake. It does not annul the Law but
allows it for the first time to come into its own. Man's efforts
are not suppressed but put into their rightful place.

That is the decisive message of the first part. God's righteousness is offered in the Gospel of Jesus Christ, and acquired

by faith. What follows in CH. IV is a kind of digression. Paul's piety, which derives from the Old Testament, sees God's rule in a long "history of salvation." How is God's decisive saving act in Jesus Christ related to His activity in the Old Covenant? This question still demands an answer, which Paul gives in CH. IV. The meditation reminds us, in many ways, of Galatians. For Paul, Abraham is not the father of works but of faith. This exposition may do a certain violence to the Old Testament but it is nonetheless a "productive misinterpretation," that is, it understands the Old Testament better than the latter understands itself and, in that respect, is superior to a purely historical interpretation of its literal contents. But Paul draws further conclusions (IV.9-25). As the father of faith Abraham belongs not to his physical posterity, which bears the outward sign of circumcision, but to all believers, Jews as well as Gentiles, circumcised as well as uncircumcised. Circumcision does not effect righteousness, but is rather only an external ratification of the righteousness already received by faith (IV.11). Is that a Jewish way of thinking? It is obvious that the opposite is the case. Not only has Paul himself been inwardly liberated from Jewish thinking by the Spirit of Christ, but he even robs Judaism of all the props of its own tradition and requisitions them for Christ. Seldom has there been a more un-Jewish way of thinking; the boldness with which the Apostle goes about it can only be understood as the result of the entry of the Divine Grace into his life.

One question requires brief consideration at the conclusion of this first section: what does Paul understand by the righteousness of God? The expression is ambiguous. It describes on the one hand God's own justice and, on the other, an attribute of man, namely his righteousness as effected by God and valid in His sight. Luther, in his translation (*Gerechtigkeit, die vor Gott gilt*: righteousness valid in God's sight) adheres one-sidedly to the second meaning. The reader would do well to allow the simple genitive "righteousness of God" to stand, instead of this circumlocution, leaving the sense to be decided in each case. The ambiguity of the expression has a deeper basis however. It is of the nature of God that He imparts His own attributes. His righteousness is perfected in the fact that he bestows it upon man. To that extent it can be equated in

content with the grace of God. This was the reforming discovery
that Luther made in his study of Rom. 1.16f. Why then does
Paul employ the concepts of "righteousness" and "justification"?
Why does he make use of these juridical-moral formulas when
he apparently reverses their meaning? The answer is, first of all,
that this is due to Paul's Jewish inheritance. He was brought
up on rabbinical conceptions, and attempts, therefore, to formulate the new subject-matter in their terms. That leads to
certain tensions and incongruities between form and content.
In fact, the Pauline doctrine of Justification can be made more
readily intelligible by the concept of adoption. This already
occurs in Jesus's preaching and Paul himself makes occasional
use of the metaphor. And yet even the juridical usage has its
own quite definite value. In spite of its incongruity it can convey one thing more clearly than can the concept of adoption,
namely, that God remains just even when he is gracious. The
rules of justice are not annulled by the rules of love, but are
fulfilled by them. Even in man's case, therefore, love is the
fulfilment of the Law. Faith does not abrogate the Law, and
justification through grace and judgment according to works
are not mutually exclusive. Sin is condemned by grace no less
than by righteousness. To forgive everything does not mean to
condone everything. The justification of the sinner does not
imply the justification of sin. God's love and God's holiness are
inseparable. The abiding value of Paul's formula "the righteousness of God," ambiguous and inadequate though it may be
in itself, lies in its vindication of these insights.

The second part of the letter (v-viii) is no less important
for Paul than the first. He is as much concerned with the
question of the possession of righteousness as with that of its
acquisition. Justification is not an end in itself; it is intended to
be no more and no less than the foundation of the Christian's
new life. Justification and sanctification are indissolubly linked
together, and God's righteousness is not only a judicial but a
creative act. God *pronounces* a man righteous and thereby *makes*
him righteous: "for he spoke, and it came to be" (Ps. xxxiii.9).
The question raised by the second part therefore runs: what
does the righteousness of God signify for the Christian? And
the answer is peace with God, sanctification, re-creation, freedom from the Law, new life and adoption by God. CHS. v-viii

do not come as an anticlimax after the heights of CH. III; on the contrary here we rise swiftly to the climax of the whole letter in CH. VIII.

Justification by faith means peace with God (v.1-11). This peace buttresses the heart against all the storms of life (v.1-5). It enables us to look out for the end undismayed. We have in fact experienced the love of God as the determining reality of our Christian life (v.5). This love has become manifest in Christ's act of reconciliation, and preserves us from the wrath of the final judgment (v.6-11). The divine love has come to oppose the empire of sin which rules the world, and proves to be the mightier power (v.12-21). As in 1 Cor. xv, Paul here places Christ and Adam in antithesis. The world of Adam, from which we all descend, is the world of sin and death. The Kingdom of Christ is the kingdom of grace and life. In relation to these two kingdoms the Law is of only subsidiary importance (v.20). It has served to enable sin to be seen for what it is—sin. To that extent it was a preparation for the Kingdom of Grace, but it could not bring this Kingdom to pass. Christ is not the second Moses but the second Adam. With Christ a new humanity begins. And yet there is more than just a parallel between the two. Christ is greater than Adam. Christianity does not teach an eternal dualism of good and evil, but subsists on God's victory over darkness. "But where sin increased, grace abounded all the more" (v.20).

The Christian has peace with God. He belongs to the new humanity. Can he rest content with this achievement? Has sin no more hold upon his life? Paul turns to these questions in CH. VI. Peace with God is not a comfortable pillow for the flesh; it means at the same time a struggle against sin. In principle, of course, the power of sin has been destroyed. But that does not release us from the daily campaign. Christ cannot live in us if Adam does not die in us (VI.1-11). Certainly Christ has done everything decisive for us in this campaign. But the fact that everything has been decided for us demands our decision. This decision must also be made good by action (VI.12-23). The new life serves the cause of righteousness (VI.19). Grace confers obligation! The Gospel has nothing in common with antinomianism, the theory which confuses freedom with licence. Paul here again strikes up the

theme of the "freedom of a Christian man." The service of
righteousness is a joyful service, which is rewarded with the free
gift of eternal life. Sin, however, repays its servants with death
(VI.23).

The whole of CH. VI is intended therefore to show that the
victory wrought by grace does not put an end to the war against
sin. The indicative "grace has appeared," involves the imperative "therefore enter into the service of grace." The
question now arises of the significance to be attached to the
Law in this fight against sin. Is it not the armoury from which
the Christian must fetch the weapons for this fight? Paul
stoutly denies this in CH. VII. By reference to the law of marriage
he seeks to prove that the Christian is legitimately free of the
Law (VII.1-6). He belongs to Christ and for him the Law is
dead. Paul's simile breaks down, of course, for it is not the Law
but the Christian who has died. Through death and re-creation
he has been freed from his previous bond. But, even though the
simile breaks down, Paul's meaning is clear. The Spirit (*i.e.*
the Spirit of God) has replaced the letter as the controlling
reality of the Christian's life (VII.6, cf. CH. VIII); these thoughts
are familiar to us from Gal. IIIff. and II Cor. III.

The Law therefore no longer dominates the Christian. There
is no question of its being a support for the Christian in his
struggle against sin. Indeed, according to vs. 5 it seems as if
the Law in fact encourages sin. The problem of the relationship
between Law and sin is summed up in the question, "could it
not be that the law itself is sin?" (VII.7). This objection, which
would make Paul an antinomian (see p. 133) must be met (VII.
7-13). The Law itself is not sin but "holy and just and good"
(VII.12). But the Law—Paul also speaks here of "commandment"—becomes the occasion of sin. At this point Paul
presents a "psychology of sin" which is assuredly based upon
his own experience. We are reminded of what we have already
heard about Paul's youth in Tarsus. Perhaps the assumption of
the Law signified an internal crisis for the young Saul (see p.
18.) It is more probable that only subsequently, as a Christian,
did Paul interpret this experience in this way. At any rate this
"psychology of sin" goes far beyond the biographical, and can
lay claim to universal validity. The "I" of Rom. VII.7-13 is not
the individual "I" of Saul-Paul; it is the "I" of each one of us.

It is not by chance that the description recalls, even in individual expressions, the story of the Fall (Gen. III), which has an equally universal validity. Sin derives not from the commandment but from the sinful propensity which is latent in man. But through the commandment this appetite awakens into consciousness and becomes a deed. To that extent the Law is the occasion of sin—a fact which everybody can observe in himself and which also underlies the narrative in Gen. III. Sin is such an uncanny power that it can even enlist the divine commandment in its service (VII.11, 13). The moment, however, that sin revives in man, his "life," this life of *naïveté*, of unbroken unity and harmony, disappears; "and I died" (VII.9f.) So the commandment, that was given for the sake of life, becomes the agent of death, so terrible is the destructive power of sin. For this reason, however, the Law cannot fulfil its task of helping the Christian to victory in his struggle against sin. How completely different this condemnation of the Law is from Kant's, for example!

Paul portrays the helplessness of the Law from yet another angle (VII.14-25). Although the Law is "spiritual," (*i.e.*, in this context, "comes from God") the natural man is "carnal." By "carnal" Paul means man in separation from God. He is also thinking of man's body as the seat of his lower instincts, but not only of his body. Paul can describe even man's higher attributes as "carnal," in so far as they are not controlled by God's Spirit. Thus all that is ungodly in man is "carnal." Being carnal, man is "sold under sin" (VII.14). For the rest Paul's description of the natural man is not entirely gloomy. The "inward man" (R.V.)—we would perhaps say the "super-ego"—affirms the law of God (VII.22). That is the most that Paul can say for man without Christ. Man can distinguish himself from his sin—but not separate himself. A terrible schism runs through human existence. Two souls dwell in his heart. Without divine succour the "flesh" triumphs in this struggle (VII.23). Paul cannot, with idealistic ardour, conceal this brutal reality. In antithesis to Kant's high-minded formula, "you can, for you ought," we here have the shattering confession: "I can will what is right, but I cannot do it" (VII.18). We must, of course, note that by "right" Paul does not mean a respectable action in the bourgeois "moral" or tragically heroic

K

sense. Paul would not deny to the natural man the possibility of such action. Here the word "right" is meant in its highest sense: "right" is that which is seen as such by God. In this sense the confession in vii.18 retains its implicit truth, which, of course, discloses itself fully only to him who diagnoses the situation of the natural man in the light of Christ. The existence of a "super-ego" in man only makes this situation the more terrible; since it succumbs in the struggle, the whole man is ultimately "flesh." The cry from the heart for redemption is the last word of the natural man (vii.24).

Of whom is Paul speaking here? Who is the "I" of vii.14ff.? The Reformers applied the verse to the Christian. The schism described runs through the Christian. He is then both justified and a sinner at the same time: "We are sinners and yet children." This interpretation is untenable, however, in view of vii.6 and the triumphal song of ch. viii. Paul is here speaking of man apart from Christ, although, certainly, as he is to be seen in the light of Christ. Neither the Jew nor the Gentile will, any more now than previously, recognise this picture automatically. It is possible to do so only in the light of faith in Christ, from which standpoint it is incontestably true. It is not a matter of making a Christian revaluation of natural reality; it is rather that only in the light of Christ is man's real situation truly perceived. Nowhere will natural philosophy enter into opposition with Paul more than at this point. It is here, in fact, that the real stumbling-block of the Gospel message lies, in relation to which all intellectual difficulties are mere quibbles. For this reason, however, the decision for or against the truth of this picture cannot be reached by intellectual means. The man who is stirred by the truth of the Gospel will recognise in it the deepest interpretation ever made of man's natural situation.

The Law cannot lead the Christian to victory in his struggle against sin. That is the conclusion drawn by ch. vii. The Christian's life, however, is subject not to the deadening claim of the Law but to the life-giving power of the divine Spirit. That is the triumphal hymn of ch. viii, in which Paul ascends to the highest peak of his confidence in salvation. In it the climax of the whole letter is reached. The chapter can be divided into four sections. Victory is ours!—that is the cry of the first section (viii.1-11); hold it fast!—that is the warning

of the second (VIII.12-17); the fulfilment is at hand!—that is
the certainty of the third section (VIII.18-31); nothing can wrest
this victory from us!—that is the jubilant note upon which the
chapter ends (VIII.31-39).

Victory is ours! That is the first note, ringing out powerfully and distinctly like a fanfare of trumpets (VIII.1-11). The
whole section is dominated by the antithesis: flesh and spirit.
But, unlike the antithesis of VII.14ff., it no longer signifies an
irreparable split. The Spirit of God is the very power which is
stronger than the flesh. Walking according to the Spirit secures
the righteousness which was impossible for the Law (VIII.3f.)
Freedom and life are the very things that specially distinguish
the Christian.

In face of this victory the power of the flesh is as good as dead
(VIII.10). Nevertheless Paul here as in VI.1ff. goes over from the
indicative to the imperative (VIII.12-17). You live in the Spirit,
therefore walk in the Spirit! The flesh is dead, therefore mortify
the flesh! You are sons, therefore do not become slaves again!

The reality of the Christian's life often seems to have little in
common with victory. The glory is still hidden under suffering
and sighing, but it will become manifest. The whole world is
bound up with the fate of man. A sigh for deliverance from
transience ("vanity": A.V.) shakes the dumb creation. A
powerful thought! The whole creation involved with man in a
fellowship of guilt and redemption! That is the Christian
"philosophy of nature" (VIII.19-22). But even the life of
believers is subject to the tension between the "no longer" and
the "not yet." Though they are sons, they have as yet to become sons. They have already received the Spirit, but only as
a kind of "down-payment," which leaves something much
greater to be expected, and, at the same time, desired (VIII.23).
So the position of the Christian in this era is necessarily one of
hope that is both joyous and patient. Paul makes a third pronouncement in addition to this: the Spirit of God Himself sighs
within us for fulfilment and thus shares in the blissful tension of
the Christian's life (VIII.26). Paul is here thinking of the
"speaking with tongues" (cf. 1 Cor. XIV). But even we are
conscious of a prayer which is obscured by our stammering
but which is nonetheless prayer. How would it be possible for
this sighing of the divine Spirit within us not to find a hearing

with God! The fulfilment is undoubtedly yet to come but it is
at hand. That is the sense of the third section, which finally
rises to the certainty of salvation expressed in vss. 28-30. God
has ordained our salvation from all eternity; therefore everything, even in this age, must minister to our salvation. A
golden chain of divine saving-acts links our Christian life, both
past and future, with eternity. From election to glorification—
that is God's way with His own.

All the sluice-gates now open for that exuberant hymn of
praise (VIII.31-39) which has no parallel in human literature.
A solemn note is sounded once again in the recollection of the
sufferings of this age (vss. 35-37), but it is swallowed up by the
jubilant certainty of salvation and the praise of redemption.
Not all the powers of this world, guilt, tribulation and death,
nor even the forces of the supernatural and demonic powers,
can tear us away from God's power. But this greatest power in
heaven and earth is none other than the love of God which has
appeared, and been bestowed upon us, in Jesus Christ.

With CH. VIII. the second part of the letter comes to a close.
We must certainly assume a pause between CHS. VIII and IX,
which accounts for the lack of any formal indication of change
of subject. Nevertheless, the third part of the letter, which now
follows (IX-XI) has its place in the whole scheme. The question:
"How is God's righteousness demonstrated in the fate of
Israel?" is not a chance one, but an essential part of the whole
letter. CH. IX.1-5 shows how deeply it moved the Apostle
himself. Perhaps he wished to demolish in advance certain
Judaistic charges circulating among the Romans regarding
an unprincipled desertion of the community of the Old
Covenant. The fate of Israel preached a solemn lesson to the
community of the New Covenant which they could not ignore.
Possibly Paul wished to say a word concerning the relationship
of Jewish Christians and Gentile Christians in the Roman
church (cf. especially XI.13-24). He does this from the loftiest
standpoint. God's righteousness operates not only in the life
of the individual but also as a governing factor in history. How
then is the rejection of Israel to be understood? That is the
question raised in the third part. Paul does not answer it all
at once, but makes several attacks upon it. It is clear to us
that he had to wrestle with the problem.

Paul begins by making an impressive testimony to the love that he has for his people (ix.1-5). He would gladly forfeit his own salvation if by so doing he could save his brethren. Israel is seen by Paul as the one nation which is the object of God's promises. But Christ has now rejected it and it stands condemned. The question therefore arises: Has God's promise thereby been invalidated? Paul denies this by first making a distinction between the natural and the spiritual Israel (ix.6-13). Israel as a race is not, even for Paul the Jew, to be identified automatically with the people of God. Here he is expressing a thought that recurs constantly in the ancient prophets (cf. Am. ix.7), and is commonplace in the New Testament (cf. Mt. iii.9, Jn. viii.39, 1 Pet. ii.9 *inter alia*). One does not belong to the people of God by natural descent but solely by virtue of God's free election. It is not our merits which determine our position in God's eyes but simply God's free appointment, who is able to elect or reject. Paul clearly stands here for the doctrine of double predestination. God can elect or reject as He will. That is an attribute of God's freedom.

But here a fresh objection immediately arises: where does God's righteousness come in? Is He not then acting arbitrarily (ix.14)? Paul does not refute this objection—he simply dismisses it (ix.14-29). Man can no more resist God than the clay can resist the potter (ix.20f.) This attitude is typical of Paul and of all biblical thought. God vindicates man, but man is not called upon to vindicate God. The concept of "theodicy" (man's vindication of God) which played such a great part in the Age of Enlightenment, and informs natural philosophy in all ages, is already the sign of an incipient decadence. Puny man desires to make himself God's master. By contrast, the doctrine of predestination categorically emphasises the unconditional sovereignty of God. God can choose His children from all races, where and as He will (ix.22-26). On the other hand, the claim to be elected does not shelter a man from condemnation. Israel cannot therefore complain. Her fate rests in God's freedom. But Paul does not content himself with this answer, for he has not yet said everything that is to be said on this score. In the following verses he does not take back anything of what has just been said, but enlarges upon it. Israel's destiny depends on submission to the free decision of God. But

this destiny is likewise based upon its own decision against
Christ and against the righteousness achieved through faith
(ix.30-x.21). Israel tries to attain it, as once Saul the Pharisee
did, by way of the Law, and does it at great cost (x.2). But she
will not recognise that Christ is the end of the Law (ix.30-x.4).
She wishes to hold her own in God's sight by means of her own
righteousness and thereby robs herself of God's grace (x.3).
Legalistic righteousness stands or falls by man's actions (x.5);
righteousness by faith exists because of God's action (x.6f.), imparted to us in the message of the Gospel (x.8-17). Israel also
has heard this message (x.18), and was able to understand it
(x.19); but she has not accepted it (x.20f.) So the fate of Israel,
although it is God's deed, is, at the same time, her own fault.

Paul could well end the third part at this point. But the
question of whether the righteousness of God is manifest in the
fate of Israel troubles him still further. So he applies himself
once more to finding a new answer (xi.1-36). The destiny of
Israel is still not complete. God's promise has not yet been
completely fulfilled, but it will be. This hope is divided, for
Paul, into three parts.

(1) Even now a section of the people have become believers,
of whom Paul himself is one (xi.1-10). It was the same in the
period of the prophets. Sometimes it appeared as if the whole
people had fallen away from God. But there was, nevertheless,
a "remnant" that had remained faithful to God. The situation
is exactly the same now (xi.1-5). Of course, this remnant
cannot attribute its constancy to its own merit, for its existence
is as much God's work as is the hardening of the others (xi.6-10).
But for that very reason it is a sure sign that God has not
rejected His people as a whole (xi.1).

(2) God's saving purpose can be detected even now in the
current rejection of Israel (xi.11-24). It is because Israel as a
people has rejected the Lord Christ that the Gospel has been
released to the Gentile world. If the people of Israel as a whole
had accepted the Gospel, Christianity would in fact have remained as nationally restricted as the religion of the Old
Testament. It would have become a new form of Judaism,
something that by definition it certainly is not. Thus the Jewish
attitude of refusal has made it easier for primitive Christianity
to find its way, in accordance with its universal character, into

the Gentile world. Israel's fall has been of profit to the world (XI.11f.) The divine significance of this event, so puzzling in itself, lies in the fact that salvation has reached the Gentiles. But that in its turn should fill Israel with envy, and thus she also will perhaps find her way to Christ. Israel's conversion would then be the end of the "history of salvation" (XI.13-16). But the Gentile Christians are not permitted to feel any arrogance (XI.17-24). In the face of Israel's situation, they, in their turn, run the risk of regarding themselves as "chosen." Paul illustrates the stupidity and danger of such an idea by the metaphor of the broken-off (Jewish) and engrafted (Gentile) branches. If God has not spared the natural branches, how much less can the engrafted branches expect to be spared (XI. 17-22). But once God has accepted the Gentiles for their faith's sake, he will then receive back the Jews, provided that they desist from their unbelief (XI.23f.)

(3) Paul arrives now at his final thought. Israel will become converted when the full number of Gentiles, as determined by God, finds the way to Christ (XI.25ff.) Paul calls this idea a "mystery" (Greek *mysterion*) that has been disclosed by God's Spirit. It is also in accordance with the Old Testament promise (XI.26f.) God has not repented of his decree. Neither Jews nor Gentiles have grounds for boasting. The history of both testifies to their disobedience towards God, but even more it testifies to God's mercy towards them (XI.28-32). The Apostle is so overwhelmed by the greatness and goodness of the divine rule, that his thinking develops into adoration (XI.33-36). The final word of Romans on the enigma of divine righteousness, in the matter of election and rejection, is a hymn of praise to God, mysterious but indisputable, who is the Origin, Lord and Goal of all history.

Two further questions must be added here:

(1) Does Paul teach double predestination as expounded, for example, by Calvin, according to which God has predestined one half of humanity to eternal blessedness, and the other half to eternal damnation? Put in this way, the question must be answered in the negative. Paul does, of course, emphasise God's absolute freedom to elect and to reject. The thoughts in CH. IX are not retracted in CH. XI. But Paul knows nothing of a division of humanity into two classes, each individual feeling

he belongs to one or other of them. There may well be election and rejection with God, but we ourselves cannot distinguish between elected and rejected. It is precisely the genuine assurance of salvation which reckons with the possibility of apostasy and thus of rejection. Predestination does not abrogate responsibility. The rejection of Israel is her own fault. The divine freedom finds its highest expression, however, in God's mercy. Paul's ideas do not make sense according to natural logic. But all natural logic must capitulate before this most mysterious of all questions. The error of every explicit doctrine of predestination lies precisely in the fact that it tries to satisfy natural logic. Paul's meditation ends in adoration. This is not only of devotional but also of theological significance. There is no other solution to this problem but adoration.

(2) Is the Christian obliged, in view of Rom. xi.25f., to believe in the ultimate conversion of Israel? This question too must be answered in the negative. Neither is Paul's picture of the end of time as presented in other passages (see note on 1 Thess. iv.13ff.) an article of faith as far as we are concerned. Certainly it must not be denied that in Rom. ix-xi something of decisive importance is said regarding the Jewish question. The religious background to the Jewish destiny is revealed here right down to its very depths. The specifically Gentile Christian danger (xi.17-24) is a live one in all ages. But the significance of Rom. ix-xi is not to be limited to the Jewish question. The reference to Israel was the contemporary form of a universal human problem. Above all, the Church in every age has a lesson to learn from the fate of Israel as it is depicted here.

We come finally to the fourth part of this powerful document (xii-xvi). It turns on the question: how does God's righteousness actually affect Christian life? After the heights of the first three parts this final part seems to descend to a lower plane. With its practical exhortations it offers nothing like the same difficulties to the understanding. But we must not forget one thing: Paul is neither a pure theorist nor merely a practical man. chs. i-xi are not vague theory but a living experience. chs. xii-xvi on the other hand are not a collection of simple practical rules for living, independent of faith, but can only be understood fully when seen against the background of chs. i-xi.

The Christian's life must be a "reasonable service" (XII.1f. R.V.); its sacrifice must accord with the nature of divine reason, the divine Spirit. The Church is a body in which all the members must co-operate (XII.3-8; cf. 1 Cor. XII.4ff.) Brotherly love, which can overcome even evil, must be supreme (XII.3-21).

Paul finds it necessary to say a special word about the Christian's relationship to the state (XIII.1-7). Revolutionary voices had evidently been heard within the Roman church, deducing from the liberty of God's children, independence of the non-Christian authorities and perhaps even revolt against them. Paul rejects this as much as he did the emancipation of women in Corinth (1 Cor. XI.1-16). The authorities are divinely appointed. Rebellion is, therefore, mutiny against God. Paul sees the dignity of the state in the fact that it is the guardian of right. In spite of many a bitter experience Paul has learned to appreciate the benefits of an ordered constitutional state. Not only the fear of punishment, but our conscience also, obliges us to be obedient to the state.

Rom. XIII spared early Christianity many an unnecessary conflict with the Roman state. It has, moreover, determined the attitude of Christianity in every century. The Lutheran ethos lies entirely along these lines. Paul speaks very definitely of the dignity of the state. However, Rom. XIII is not the only word on this matter. Jesus's distinction between the Kingdom of God and the kingdoms of this world is valid also for Paul (cf. 1 Cor. VI.1ff.) Rom. XIII does not answer all the questions raised by public and political life as we know it. Paul speaks about the "authorities," for the state as the expression of the national and racial will is unknown to him. Rom. XIII presupposes the constitutional state; is every despotism to be described as "authority" in this sense? Paul eschews the Christian revolution; but does there not exist the right of armed rebellion against a government which violates its moral and national obligations? The Bible is not a Law-book of universal validity; this must be borne in mind even in relation to Rom. XIII. Every age is faced with its own problems, but it can, in the process, learn from the spirit of earlier decisions. In this fact lie the limitations, but also the importance, of Rom. XIII.

The commandment to love is the supreme law governing relationships with the world as well as within the Church

(XIII.8-10). The day of Christ is approaching, and this lays us
under the obligation to walk in the light (XIII.11-14. cf. note on
I Thess. v.5ff.) Rom. XIII.13 was decisive for Augustine's conversion (see p. 2).

In the Roman church as much as in the Corinthian church
(cf. I Cor. VIII-X) there was the problem of the "weak" and the
"strong." By the "weak" in this case was probably meant a
Jewish-Christian minority. It was not the abstention from meat
sacrificed to idols but the observance of definite food-regulations which was under dispute. Rom. XIV.1-15 is intended to
show the right way out of these quite concrete difficulties.
The supreme principle is this: our whole life and even our
dying belong to the Lord. To Him both strong and weak are
equally responsible; therefore they must not judge one another.
Christ is Judge over us all (XIV.1-12). Instead of judging we
should show consideration for the convictions and conscience
of the other (XIV.13-23), especially as God's Kingdom is not
simply a matter of food-regulations (XIV.17). But whoever acts
contrary to his conscience is guilty of sin (XIV.23). Paul regards
himself as one of the strong (XV.1). They should bear with the
weak, just as Christ bore with our weakness. We are told to
be united and have fellowship with one another (XV.1-7). If
the antithesis of Jew and Gentile has been overcome in Jesus
Christ, then perhaps we must tolerate the antithesis of strong
and weak (XV.8-13).

What follows in XV.14-33 is personal information of which we
have already had occasion to speak in our historical introduction to Romans. Paul is anxious about his impending
journey to Jerusalem and asks the church to pray for his safety
(XV.30-33). Phoebe, the deaconess from Cenchreae (see p. 87),
conveyed the letter to Rome (XVI.1f.) The many greetings
addressed to a church with which the Apostle was unacquainted
do not necessitate isolation of CH. XVI. Paul would purposely
have emphasised the personal relationships which already
existed between him and the church, and which are easily
explained by the traffic in those days between east and west.
The only un-Pauline feature is the doxology which, as is
evident from the style of the Greek text (XVI.25-27), was added
later. This addition was merely a liturgical necessity arising
out of the fact that the letter had to be read publicly, in church.

# PAUL THE PRISONER

WE broke off the description of the Apostle's career at his eventual arrival in Jerusalem (Acts XXI.17; see p. 94). His reception by James and the elders of the mother church was not over-friendly. One suspects difficulties arising from the fact that Paul was generally regarded as an apostate, because they could not accept his unlegalistic Christianity. Paul was required to clear himself of this suspicion by making a vow. That was a tremendous demand to make of the Apostle to the Gentiles. The fact that he made it, nevertheless, shows how much the unity of Christendom meant to him. It was one of the most difficult decisions of his career (Acts XXI.17-26).

Catastrophe, however, was inevitable. Jews from Asia, presumably from Ephesus, who had already lain in wait for Paul on an earlier occasion, accused him in front of the excited temple-crowd of having brought an uncircumcised man into the inner court. This was considered a terrible act of blasphemy and was forbidden on pain of death. It is impossible to exaggerate the fanaticism of a Jewish crowd. Only the intervention of the Roman garrison, which was always reinforced at festival times, was able to prevent Paul from being lynched. He was temporarily taken into protective custody, but, at his own request, he was allowed to address the people. The familiar Aramaic tones silenced the crowd for a while (Acts XXI.27-40). Paul recounted his conversion, and he appealed for the understanding of his compatriots (Acts XXII.1-21). But what did that matter to fanatics? The key-word "Gentiles" sufficed to unleash a new frenzy. It was decided to extract his confession by torture—a concession to the mob similar to that made by Pilate. But Paul foiled this by declaring himself to be a Roman citizen. Under Roman surveillance he now had to answer for himself next day before the Supreme Council (Acts XXII.22-30), and in course of this he proved himself a clever tactician. He caused something of a sensation at the meeting by bringing the discussion to bear upon a Jewish

domestic controversy. So once again he was taken into temporary custody (Acts XXIII.1-11), for the Jews did not want to
let their prey escape. Forty men solemnly pledged themselves
to an attempt on Paul's life, but the plot leaked out through
a nephew of Paul's. The garrison commander felt the matter
to be so serious that he sent Paul under a strong escort to the
residence of Felix, the governor at Caesarea (Acts XXIII.12-25).

The first hearing under Felix, at which the accusers from
Jerusalem appeared, again produced no result (Acts XXIV.1-23).
The Apostle's private discussions with this mentally unstable
governor are highly significant psychologically, although for the
rest, they came to nothing. And now began the endless delaying
of his trial (Acts XXIV.24-27), which was the hardest thing for
Paul. Felix's successor, Porcius Festus, was made of different
metal. There was still something of the old Roman legal sense
in him. Another hearing took place. Paul would no longer
acknowledge the authority of the Supreme Council. As a
Roman citizen he had the right of appeal to the Emperor, and
Paul made use of this right. Further proceedings in Caesarea
appeared hopeless, and he did not wish to be handed over to the
spiritual court in Jerusalem. The only way out was an appeal
to Caesar, and Festus granted him this (Acts XXV.1-12).

Luke has described for us one last scene in Caesarea. It is
the visit of Herod Agrippa II (the great-grandson of Herod the
Great) and his famous and infamous sister, Bernice, who later
became the mistress of the emperor Titus. Festus takes advantage of the presence of these "experts" in Jewish affairs to
let Paul have his say once more (Acts XXV.13-XXVI.32). Three
worlds confront each other here, represented by the religiously
inclined but dilettante Herod, the fiery defendant Paul and,
between them, the wholly materialistic but honest Roman!
This is all described by Luke with fine psychological insight.
Festus is convinced by this time of Paul's political harmlessness,
but the appeal to Caesar has been made and it must be carried
through.

Now began the Apostle's journey to Rome. How differently
he had imagined it would be! He was now to enter the world
capital as the prisoner of Christ. It was already autumn and
the voyage not without its hazards under the conditions of those
days. However, they managed to reach Crete without over-

much difficulty (Acts xxvii.1-8), but it was inadvisable to continue the voyage any further. Nevertheless, as the harbour was not suitable for spending the winter in, the captain decided to go on, against the advice of Paul, whose experience of many voyages qualified him to voice an opinion on the matter. The consequences were dire indeed. The description of the storm at sea (Acts xxvii.9-44) is, in the opinion of a modern expert, "the most valuable nautical document that has been preserved for us from antiquity; it can only have been compiled by an eyewitness." It is unnecessary to recount it in detail here; let the reader turn it up and feel the impact of it for himself! The human greatness of the Apostle, rooted in his faith, stands out against the tempestuous background; it also stands at the centre of the events on Malta, where the shipwrecked company eventually landed, after a fortnight's struggle against the full fury of the elements (xxviii.1-10).

After wintering for three months in the gentle climate of Malta they were able to resume the voyage. The new ship was adorned with the figurehead of the Dioscuri, Castor and Pollux. We would gladly accompany Paul in our imagination on his journey along the coast of southern Italy. Syracuse, the Straits of Messina, Naples, Puteoli, a host of glittering names passes before our eyes in the account in Acts, names unforgettable for any who have ever been privileged to make the same journey. They disembarked at Puteoli and continued the six or seven days' journey to Rome on foot. At Capua they joined the famous Via Appia which ran from Rome to Brundisium (Brindisi). The church in Rome had heard of the Apostle's arrival; they sent two deputations to meet him, one as far as the Forum of Appius (forty miles from Rome) and the other as far as Three Taverns (thirty miles from Rome). We can easily imagine how heartened Paul was by the welcome he received from the brethren (Acts xxviii.11-16).

"And so we came to Rome" (Acts xxviii.14). By its very brevity, this simple statement suggests the momentousness of this step. Paul was not confined in anything like strict custody in Rome; he was able to move about very freely under the supervision of a soldier and lived in his own lodgings (Acts xxviii.16, 30f.) Once again he tried to come to an understanding with the synagogue (Acts xxviii.17-29). The Jewish community in Rome at the time of Nero was numerous (approximately thirty thousand) and influential; it even had connexions with the imperial household. Paul was concerned that he should not be regarded simply as an apostate; it was for the sake of Israel's Messianic hope that he now stood as a prisoner before the heads of the synagogue (Acts xxviii.20). The controversy proceeded as was only to be expected. History had already spoken; the separation of Christianity and Judaism had already become fact: salvation had come to the Gentiles. Paul, the apostle of the Gentiles, preached the Gospel in the world-capital "unhindered." The road from Jerusalem to Rome had been covered; east and west were now one in Christ. The world-embracing achievement of the greatest missionary of all time was on the verge of fulfilment. Luke's account breaks off at this point. The theme of Acts, which was how the Gospel came to the Gentiles, has been expounded.

# THE LETTERS FROM PRISON

AMONG Paul's "letters from prison" are the letters to the Philippians, Colossians, Ephesians, and Philemon. The exact circumstances of their composition are veiled in mystery, and the genuineness of Colossians and Ephesians is also controversial.

That Philippians was written from prison is an undisputed fact (1.7, 13, 17). But what imprisonment are we dealing with here? We know from Acts of the imprisonments in Caesarea and Rome. The references to the "praetorium" (1.13, mg.) and "Caesar's household" (IV.22) have, for centuries, been adduced in support of its composition in Rome. But every residence of an imperial governor in the provinces was called the "praetorium," and the imperial slaves in the provincial capitals also belonged to "Caesar's household." Other facts militate against Rome's claim. The lively exchange of news portrayed here is hardly conceivable in view of the great distance from Philippi. The proposed itinerary in Phil. 1.26 and II.24 does not correspond with that in Rom. xv.24, 28. The bitter attack upon the Judaisers (Phil. III) no longer fits in with the Roman period. It has therefore been assumed that it was composed at Caesarea, but a great deal remains obscure if we accept this. A more recent suggestion has been Ephesus. Certainly Acts does not tell of an imprisonment there; but in view of II Cor. XI.23ff. we must recognise that Acts is an incomplete record. An imprisonment in Ephesus is therefore perfectly possible. Philippians would then fall in the period between Galatians and I Corinthians. But even the Ephesus theory does not offer a completely convincing solution.

The letter to the Philippians is set in a cordial and personal key. The church at Philippi, founded on the second missionary journey (Acts XVI.12ff.), has cheered Paul with a gift of money. The letter is his thanks for it. The bearer of the contribution, Epaphroditus, is also the bearer of the letter (II.25, IV.14, 18, II.28). Specific details of particular abuses in the church are not given. The warning against Judaism (III) is probably based more upon Paul's general anxiety than upon circumstances in that particular church. On the face of it, the letter gives expression only to Paul's joy and gratitude. But the manner in which he does this is what constitutes the uniqueness and greatness of this letter.

The personal, epistolary character of the document is evident from the lack of arrangement. The initial greeting and thanksgiving for the church (1.1-11) is followed by news of the physical and spiritual state of the Apostle (1.12-26); it resounds with confidence. Paul's imprisonment has served only to extend the Gospel (1.12-14); his rivals, insincere though they are, must inevitably preach Christ—he cannot be referring here to false teachers—(1.15-18); his trial will turn out well. Paul, in spite of his longing for death, would gladly remain alive, in order to be of further use (1.19-26). Exhortations to the church now follow (1.27-11.18). They must, above all, live in harmony: this is possible only when everyone thinks not of himself but of others. Their great example in this is Christ Himself (11.5-11). They will therefore create their salvation only when they realise that God alone can create it for them. Here again (11.12f.) we encounter the unity of indicative and imperative with which we are familiar from the letter to the Romans. In this way they will give the Apostle the greatest joy (11.14-18). The chapter concludes with news of Timothy and Epaphroditus.

In CH. III the mood suddenly changes—probably owing to a pause in dictation. Paul condemns most bitterly the machinations of the Judaisers. They are so proud of their privileges but Paul can boast of just the same ones (III.1-16; cf. II Cor. XI.16ff.) Yet he has renounced everything for the sake of Christ, in order to attain righteousness by faith, even though he is not yet perfect (III.7-14). The Philippians should emulate him in this respect. They should not be burdened by material considerations, for their "citizenship" (R.V.) is in Heaven (III.15-21). This is followed once again by a series of individual exhortations (IV.1-9). Who the "yokefellow" (IV.3) is we do not know. The nearness of the Lord both in the present and in the future bestows peace and joy (IV.4-7). The letter concludes with renewed thanks for the Philippians' gift, as considerate as it was cordial, and more greetings (IV.10-23).

For the letter to the Colossians, Rome, Caesarea and Ephesus are all possible places of composition. In favour of Ephesus there is its geographical proximity to Colossae. But the letter's form and content do not fit in with the Ephesus period, which was taken up with the struggle against Judaism. Militating against Caesarea, on the other hand, is the fact that the runaway slave, Onesimus, would hardly have strayed in that direction (IV.9). So the old assumption that it was written in Rome is still the most probable.

The church was not founded by Paul but by the Colossian Epaphras (I.7, IV.12; and see above, p. 91). It was being threatened at the time of the letter by false teachers (II.4, 8, 16), who were demanding the observance of feasts and food-laws (II.16, 21) combined with strict asceticism. Above all, however, they represented an angelology of the kind associated with what is called gnosticism ("philosophy," II.8), meaning a speculative religious system which spread from the East, made up of the most diverse elements. These false teachers had no connexion with Judaisers; they demanded neither circumcision nor any other form of strict legalism. Paul is here campaigning not against Judaism, but against a form of religious syncretism found in late antiquity. The veneration of spiritual powers serves to draw one's gaze away from the central figure, from Christ, whose Cross stands for victory over these powers.

Many doubt whether Paul is the auther of Colossians. Its language, vocabulary and sentence construction have many peculiarities, and its style is clumsy. In its pronouncements on Christology it goes beyond anything in the earlier letters. These observations might well cast doubt upon Paul's authorship, but do not rule out the possibility altogether.

The letter to Colossae has two parts, a doctrinal (I and II) and a practical (III and IV). As usual, he begins with a salutation, thanksgiving and intercession (I.1-12), followed by some direct and powerful statements regarding Christ's position as divine mediator within the total cosmos (I.13-20). Christ is Lord also of the world of spirits (I.16, 20); this is stressed not without reference to the false teachers. The particular concern of Colossians is the *cosmic* significance of Christ. The Colossians have also experienced the salvation wrought by Christ (I.21-23). Paul therefore rejoices in his ministry even when undergoing suffering, which he interprets in mystical fashion as a continuance of the sufferings of Christ (1.24-29). But Paul cannot conceal his anxiety for the church and its neighbour in Laodicea. They must beware of false doctrine (II.1-23); the Gospel is the true wisdom (II.3-9); Christ is victor over the spiritual powers (II.10-15); He has released us from bondage to all ritual and ascetic precepts (II.16-23).

The second part (III and IV) consists mainly of exhortations. The ethic of the Christian life has as its motto: You have died and risen with Christ. The new life of the Christian is as much "hid in God" as the life of the risen Christ. All the more, therefore, put on the new man! Have love for one another! Do everything in the name of the Lord Jesus (III.1-17)! The Christian "house-tables" (see p. 113) are drawn up in the same spirit (III.18-IV.1). Exhortations to prayer and a wise attitude towards non-Christians (IV.2-6), together with personal news and greetings (IV.7-18), conclude this part and also the letter, which, whether genuine or not, has its own special character. Whenever people start talking about the cosmic significance of Christ (as in anthroposophy), this letter is a cry of warning against losing the essence of the Gospel in fantastic speculation.

The letter to the Ephesians is very closely linked with the letter to the Colossians in that it presupposes the same situation. Paul is in prison (Eph. III.1, VI.19ff.) Tychicus is the bearer of both letters (Col. IV.7f., Eph. VI.21f.) The linguistic peculiarities of Colossians are even more marked in Ephesians. The accumulating of synonymous expressions and a certain liturgical solemnity are the chief characteristics of the style of Ephesians. The theme is akin to that of Colossians; there it was the cosmic Christ; here it is the cosmic significance of the Church itself. If the authenticity of Colossians is in doubt, that of Ephesians is even more so.

One thing, at any rate, is certain: Ephesians was not written to the Ephesians. The words "at Ephesus" (1.1mg) are missing from the best ancient manuscripts; the superscription dates from a much later period. If the letter was written by Paul, it could not, on grounds of subject-matter, have been destined for Ephesus. In no church had Paul stayed so long as in Ephesus (see pp. 89ff.), yet the letter contains no personal references, no greeting, and indeed it is obvious that the writer and his readers are not acquainted with each other (1.15,

III.2ff.) It also lacks that warm and cordial note that we find in all of Paul's other letters. Are we perhaps dealing in Ephesians with the "letter from Laodicea" mentioned in Col. IV.16? It is an old and attractive idea. But it does not explain how a letter to Laodicea became a letter to Ephesus. Even if we accept its genuineness we cannot but wonder at the impersonal tone of the document. How very different Colossians is in this respect, even though Paul had only second-hand knowledge of this church! The best explanation is as follows: the "letter" is a circular letter to several churches, handed on from place to place, with a new address superimposed each time. It could easily have received the title "Ephesians" when the apostolic letters were later collected together, especially as there would certainly have been a copy in the church at Ephesus.

Can we, however, continue to accept the belief that Paul wrote the letter? This question must, we feel, be answered in the negative. The main reason lies in the fact that Ephesians speaks in a totally different language from the genuinely Pauline letters. At a pinch it is possible to explain the linguistic peculiarities of Colossians by reference to the expressions used by Paul's opponents, but not so with Ephesians, which betrays even more marked linguistic dissimilarities from Paul's authentic letters than does Colossians. Paul usually speaks with lively excitement, pressing on from idea to idea, but Ephesians is slow, solemn, liturgically formal, and almost sluggish and tedious in expression. The way of thinking found in Ephesians is not entirely un-Pauline; it could be interpreted as a further development of the Paulinism with which we are already familiar. Nevertheless, it is scarcely conceivable that an expression like the "holy apostles" (III.5) was Paul's (cf. Gal. II.6ff.), for it is typical of a man of the second generation. The connexion between Ephesians and Colossians militates more against, than on behalf of, the authenticity of Ephesians. Admittedly we find in Ephesians a strong approximation to the vocabulary of Colossians, but the phrases, though they sound similar, are used in a different sense. In Colossians they have a Christological significance, but here they are transferred to the Church.

The ancient world knew nothing of copyright as we understand it. It was quite permissible for a man to sign his own works with some famous name: there are plenty of instances of

this. Ephesians would be an example of this. This conclusion
should in no way depress us; on the contrary, we should be
glad that in the apostolic era there were, in addition to the
known, also unknown, great men.

The letter can be divided, like Colossians, into a predominantly doctrinal (I-III), and a predominantly practical (IV-VI),
half. There is also the peculiar (and un-Pauline) fact that
the doctrinal exposition precedes the thanksgiving and intercession (cf. 1.3, 1.15).

The letter begins with a powerful introduction (1.3-14). In
the Greek text these verses are a single sentence. It has a
perceptibly trinitarian construction. After the announcement
of the theme in vs. 3, vss. 4-6 tell of the election by God, vss.
7-10 of the redemption by Christ, vss. 11-14 of the unity of those
chosen and redeemed in the Holy Spirit. The introduction is
couched in rhythmic style with conscious artistry, and is
followed by the prayer to God that its readers may be granted a
full knowledge of salvation (1.15-23). The crux of the letter is
reached in vs. 23; the Church as the body of Christ. Salvation
has come to the Ephesians and has effected a revolution in them
(II.1-10). They were formerly Gentiles, but now, through
Christ's act of reconciliation, they have been welded with the
Jewish Christians in one unified Church (II.11-22). The real
concern of Ephesians becomes clear at this point: the unity of
Gentile Christians and Jewish Christian in one Church as the
body of Christ. The much-quoted phrase "he is our peace"
(II.14) is to be interpreted in this sense. There is an interesting
comparison in this connexion between Col. II.14 and Eph. II.15.
In the former the Law is the power which opposes man's
salvation because it testifies against him; here, in Eph. II.15,
however, the Law is the dividing wall which separates Israel
from the Gentile world. The shift in emphasis, in spite of the
similarity of expression, is clear. The theme of Ephesians is thus
the fruits of Paul's life-work. How he had striven for the unity
of the two groups in Christ! The incorporation of the Gentiles
into God's plan of salvation—that is the secret "mystery" that
has been revealed to the Apostle, in the service of which he
labours and suffers (III.1-13). Once again the much-interrupted
intercession is resumed and the first part brought thus to its
conclusion (III.14-21).

The "practical" section is again dominated by the thought of unity. Different gifts are certainly bestowed upon individuals, as is emphasised by the quotation in IV.8 together with its exposition in IV.9f. There are many gifts but there is one Spirit, since we are also one body (IV.1-16). As in Colossians, ethics are subordinated to the thought of the new man created in the image of Christ (IV.17-24). This new creation must be manifested in quite practical and concrete matters (IV.25-V.21). Christians must be children of the light, because that is indeed what they are (V.8f.); here we have renewed echoes of Rom. XIII.11f. and 1 Thess. v.5ff. The antithesis of wine and spirit (v.18) recalls Acts II.13ff., and also has religio-historical associations such as are seen in the cult of Dionysius. Biblical piety rejects religious intoxication and professes an alert spirituality. The Christian "house-tables" are here expounded at length (V.22-VI.9). The Catholic view of marriage as a sacrament is based upon V.32; the Greek word *mysterion* (secret) is rendered in the Latin Bible by *sacramentum*. The letter comes to a powerful close in the metaphor of spiritual armour (VI.10-17; cf. Rom. XIII.12, 1 Thess. v.8). This warlike preparation is, of course, for a peaceful purpose and leads only to prayer—even for the writer of the letter, who, with a suprising *volte-face*, comes, in conclusion, to speak of himself (VI.18-24). Even if it is improbable that this letter originated with Paul himself, it has, quite rightly, by virtue of its powerful subject-matter, been adopted as part of the New Testament writings.

Paul's brief letter to Philemon is a purely personal document. Philemon had become a Christian through Paul (vs. 19) and presumably lived in Colossae, since his slave, Onesimus, hailed from there (Col. IV.9). This slave, who bore the lovely name of "Useful" had become a real "good-for-nothing" in his master's eyes (vs. 11). He had probably robbed him (vs. 18), and thereafter absconded (vs. 15). In his flight he had found refuge with Paul (in Rome? Ephesus? Caesarea?), and had been converted by him to Christianity (vs. 10). Paul would gladly have kept him, as he had come to hold him very dear (vss. 12f.) But he regarded it as his duty to send him back to his old master (vs. 14). The letter is one of recommendation (vss. 15ff.) to take with him. At the same time it intimates Paul's impending visit (vs. 22). Vs. 22 makes it seem unlikely that there was any imprisonment in distant Rome.

If we read this short letter quietly line by line we shall be amazed at the inner delicacy and affection that Paul, this powerful campaigner, possessed; for their sake alone this private letter would be severely missed from the Biblical canon. But at the same time it is a beautiful and true-to-life testimony to the way in which Christianity—although it did not drastically alter ancient institutions (Onesimus remained a slave; cf. 1 Cor. vii.21 r.v. mg.)—nevertheless transformed them from within; and that is the greater achievement. The noblest humanity and Christian love are, in this most delightful of all Paul's letters, blended into one.

# PAUL'S END

THE conclusion of Acts has occasioned much learned debate. Even when we say that the theme which Acts set itself has been expounded, the question still remains: why did Luke stop here? Why did he not say anything more about the end of Paul's life? Did he intend to write a third book, and was he prevented from doing so by circumstances of one kind and another? Or did he not know anything certain about Paul's end? Or did he not live to see it? The questions can be multiplied; but we shall concern ourselves only with that regarding Paul's end.

This problem cannot be solved with any certainty by reference to sources. The New Testament gives us no definite information on this score. If we could maintain with any precision that the so-called *Pastoral Epistles* (I and II Timothy, Titus) were written by Paul himself, then, of course, we should go a long way towards finding a solution. But the situations that they presuppose cannot actually be fitted in with what we know of Paul's life. According to I Tim. 1.3 Paul has made a journey to Macedonia and hopes soon to visit Timothy in Ephesus (I Tim. III.14, IV.13). The letter to Titus is addressed to Crete (Tit. 1.5); Paul is on his way to Nicopolis on the west coast of Greece (Tit. III.12). The choice of place indicates that he intends to go further west. With the writing of II Timothy, Paul is again in prison (1.8, 16, II.9), and that in Rome (1.17); public activity is forbidden him (1.17); his martyrdom is imminent (IV.6-8). We cannot therefore be dealing in this imprisonment with the arrest in Acts XXVIII.16ff. This results in the following picture: after two year's imprisonment in Rome (Acts XXVIII.30) he was set free. He then probably made the planned journey to Spain mentioned in Rom. xv.24, 28. This agrees with the evidence of I Clement (*c.* A.D. 96) which tells (CH. v.5-7) how Paul reached the boundary of the west before suffering martyrdom in Rome (see p. 1). It is very improbable that this testimony, coming so soon after the Apostle's death, would have been deduced solely from Rom. xv. It is probably based on

historical knowledge. According to the evidence of the Pastoral
Epistles, therefore, Paul might have travelled eastwards once
more after his first Roman imprisonment and then back to the
West, falling foul of a second Roman imprisonment in the
process.

This tradition may be historical even if the Pastoral Epistles
are not authentic. However, there are three reasons why we
must assume the latter:

(1) The Pastoral Epistles profess to be occasional letters, but
are not. Why should Paul give his familiar and long-standing
colleagues such general information regarding the nature of
Christianity (1 Tim. II.4, Tit. III.4 *inter alia*)? Timothy is believed capable of some remarkable things: slackness of morals
(1 Tim. I.19, IV.16, VI.11), covetousness (1 Tim. VI.5-10), youthful lusts (II Tim. II.22). Can this be the same man whom Paul
gave such a glorious character in Phil. II.20ff.? None of this is
addressed in actual fact to Timothy at all. The Pastoral
Epistles are not occasional letters to definite individuals, but
ecclesiastical ordinances with general rules for the life of the
Church and particular precepts for the heads of congregations
(*i.e.*, *episkopoi*).

(2) The language is not Paul's, a fact which is admitted by
those who hold with its authenticity; but they speak of Paul's
"later style." This explanation is far too superficial to be convincing, and gives a remarkable picture of Paul's stylistic
development. Starting with the dialectical and excited style of
the great letters the road proceeds by way of the liturgical and
ponderous language of Ephesians and Colossians to the simple
language of the Pastoral Epistles. Such a development is improbable, to say the least. For the rest, the linguistic peculiarities of the Pastoral Epistles can only be demonstrated by
reference to the Greek text, and we cannot go into this here.

(3) The climate of ideas in the Pastoral Epistles is different
from that of Paul's, and is typical of post-Pauline literature.
A similar climate can be found in 1 Clement (*c.* A.D. 96).
Instead of a "being-in-Christ," faith becomes more and more a
"regarding-as-true," an intellectual conviction of the correctness of Christian doctrine. Such expressions as "sound . . .
faith" (Tit. I.13, II.2), or "sound doctrine" (1 Tim. I.10, VI.3,
Tit. II.7f.) would have seemed foreign to Paul. The second

characteristic feature of post-apostolic literature is the emphasis upon good works (cf. 1 Tim. II.10, v.10, vi.18, II Tim. II.21, III.17, Tit. II.14). This corresponds with the praise of the good conscience (1 Tim. 1.5, 19, III.9, IV.2, Tit. 1.15). Of course, Paul always relates the imperative to the indicative. But what he makes good in a profound way by reference to the Death and Resurrection of Christ is here taken for granted as being a compatibility that is self-evident. Paul's weighty doctrine of Justification here assumes "catholic" lines with its straightforward juxtaposition of "faith and good works." A third characteristic detail is the receding of the eschatological hope; one must be prepared for the future days. Hand in hand with this goes a stress upon the ordinances of Church and creation (1 Tim. II.2, 15, IV.1, II Tim. IV.3). All this is not intended to cast a slur upon the Pastoral Epistles; this development was probably historically necessary. But the disparity between this and Paul is clear. One can detect little of the volcanic nature of Paul's letters in the Pastoral Epistles. They are all the more important for a Church which had to live in the world as it is; and many a passage in them still has a great deal to say to our own generation.

Even though the Pastoral Epistles do not originate from Paul, the historical situation that they presuppose rests upon sound tradition. But there is no certainty on this score. The only definite evidence we have is of Paul's death as a martyr in Rome (1 Clem. v). As a Roman citizen Paul would have been put to the sword. The majestic Basilica of St. Paul "without the walls" stands upon the site of his tomb. As to when his martyrdom took place we are in complete ignorance. Did it fall in the period before the Neronic persecution? Or was Paul one of its many victims? If we regard a second Roman imprisonment as probable, then we must conjecture an even later date. This offers us a margin from about A.D. 63 to A.D. 67; Paul would then have been somewhere in his sixties. Be that as it may, the fact of the martyrdom itself is well attested. We might almost say that this Christ-dedicated life could not have ended otherwise than in death for its Lord.

\*　　　\*　　　\*

This life now lies before us, a life of uniquely dramatic weight and tension. At the beginning of our account we heard the voices for and against Paul. The reader must now decide for himself on which side he stands. The Apostle's work needs no defence from me; it speaks for itself. It follows from our account that this work does not lead away from Christ but, on the contrary, was the first vehicle of Christ's work to the world. Our account is not intended to be a glorification of the Apostle. We would have been rendering a very poor service to the man who put "boasting" so far away from him. It is intended to do justice to the truth, in accordance with the Apostle's own words: "We cannot do anything against the truth, but only for the truth" (II Cor. XIII.8). On our attitude towards the truth, whose divine meaning is ultimately Christ Himself (Jn. XIV.6), depends our attitude to the most powerful witness to Him that the world has ever known.